Bill
Pigo
(206) 296-5691

BALANCING
ACT

Joan Kofodimos

BALANCING ACT

How managers
can integrate
successful
careers
and fulfilling
personal lives

Jossey-Bass Publishers
San Francisco

Substantial discounts on bulk quantities of Jossey-Bass books are available to corporations, professional associations, and other organizations. For details and discount information, contact the special sales department at Jossey-Bass Inc., Publishers. (415) 433-1740; Fax (415) 433-0499.

For sales outside the United States, contact Maxwell Macmillan International Publishing Group, 866 Third Avenue, New York, New York 10022.

Manufactured in the United States of America

10% POST
CONSUMER
W A S T E

Library of Congress Cataloging-in-Publication Data

Kofodimos, Joan R.
    Balancing act : how managers can integrate successful careers and fulfilling personal lives / Joan Kofodimos.
      p.   cm.—(The Jossey-Bass management series)
    Includes bibliographical references and index.
    ISBN 1-55542-508-9 (alk. paper)
    1. Executives—Psychology. 2. Workaholics. 3. Quality of work life. 4. Work and family. 5. Self-realization. 6. Executives—United States—Case studies. I. Title. II. Series.
HD38.2.K63   1993
658.4'09—dc20

93-4589
CIP

FIRST EDITION
HB Printing   10 9 8 7 6 5 4 3 2 1   *Code 9366*

The Jossey-Bass
Management Series

CONTENTS

LIST OF EXERCISES

PREFACE

Career-oriented men and women are having more difficulty balancing their professional and personal lives in the 1990s than they ever have before. Managers, professionals, and entrepreneurs of the new generation are voicing an increased desire for success and fulfillment in both work and personal life. Such balance can be difficult to achieve, particularly in a business environment that presents continually increasing demands for excellence and commitment at work.

The term *balance,* as I use it in *Balancing Act,* refers to a satisfying, healthy, and productive life that includes work, play, and love; that integrates a range of life activities with attention to self and to personal and spiritual development; and that expresses a person's unique wishes, interests, and values. It contrasts with the imbalance of a life dominated by work, focused on satisfying external requirements at the expense of inner development, and in conflict with a person's true desires.

Managers and those who seek to help them have yet to find workable solutions to the problem of imbalance. Attempts to deal with the issue are usually carried out in a piecemeal fashion. Self-help writers suggest coping mechanisms, stress management strategies, and methods of making time for nonwork activities. Management writers refer to the inherent trade-offs between career success and personal life satisfaction. Work-family researchers outline strategies and tactics for creating "family-friendly" workplaces.

Proponents of the recovery perspective describe overwork as an addiction, rooted in family dysfunction. But each of these approaches addresses just a slice of the problem.

The phenomenon of imbalance is not just a result of work load and time pressure—other types of imbalance lie beneath the surface and contribute to the dominance of work over personal life. The multiple levels of imbalance result from the interplay between individual character or personality on one hand and organizational and social forces on the other. Imbalance, in fact, is embedded in the American social character—it is an expression of the primacy of work and the perceived virtue of a mastery-oriented approach to living.

In my conversations with hundreds of managers, I have found that the issue of balance is an emotional one—it is a crucial dilemma close to their hearts. Because it is so deeply rooted, those individuals who seek balance will have to pursue fundamental changes in their approach to life and in the functioning of their organizations.

Purpose of the Book

In *Balancing Act* I take a comprehensive and deep look at the range of personal, organizational, and social forces that underlie managers' experiences of life imbalance. The model I will describe is based on ten years of research, organizational consulting, management training, self-reflection, and learning from others' work. I will present actual case information from the lives of the managers I have studied. Although the identities of the managers and the details of their lives have been disguised and several of the case stories presented are actually composites, I have sought to preserve the essence of their characters and life dilemmas. (For a description of the research studies, please see the Appendix.)

Thus, the purpose of the book is to describe the root causes of imbalance, to reveal the implicit model of success on which individual development and organizational functioning are currently based, and to propose an alternative way of living and experiencing success that is consistent with life balance and organizational health. Specifically, I hope to give readers who are dissatisfied with the structure of their own lives a new and deeper insight into the reasons why work takes over—reasons having to do with their own inner needs as well as with organizational pressures. I hope to rouse motivation to change by demonstrating the costs of imbalance for managers and for organizations. And, finally, I will provide guidelines and tools that can help managers achieve more satisfying professional and personal lives and that can equip them to create organizations that integrate human development with business effectiveness as equal and mutually supportive goals.

Who Should Read This Book?

Balancing Act is written primarily for managers, executives, and entrepreneurs who are concerned with the quality of their lives, who are frustrated with spending the bulk of their time and energy working, whose work keeps them up at night, who do not see their family or friends as much as they would like to, and whose time spent in nonwork activities feels like a pale shadow of the gratification to be had at work.

This book is also for practitioners—executive development specialists, human resource managers, organizational consultants— who plan or facilitate executives' and managers' development or who are involved with organizational change, effectiveness, and design.

These two populations—readers interested in their own life balance and those who help others with balance issues—overlap substantially. Human resource practitioners and other helping professionals often face balance dilemmas in their own lives; it is especially important, therefore, that they deal with these dilemmas in order to better help both themselves and others.

By the same token, executives and managers who learn how to make their own lives more satisfying will ultimately affect the lives of fellow workers and create organizational cultures that support balance.

A Caveat

The ideas in *Balancing Act* are based on research data. However, the implications I present go beyond what can be narrowly deduced from the data. Thus, I would like to clarify at the outset where data-based inference ends and thoughtful speculation begins.

This book is largely about men, the group that currently dominates corporate management. From 1984 to 1988, my research involved intensive biographical study of the character structure of male executives; thus when I talk about the inner forces that lead to the dominance of work in managers' lives, I am referring to male managers' character structure, socialization, drives, needs, and so on. In recent years, my research focus has broadened to look at how organizations themselves foster imbalance; thus I will also discuss the impact of organizational forces on men and women alike. I will address the similarities between the character structure of male managers and the values and beliefs of organizations—values and beliefs that constitute a male model of success—and I will discuss how this male model creates pressures and tensions for women, as well as for men, who work in those organizations. As the ongoing research program of which this book is a part continues to unfold, I hope to look more intensively at the inner force shaping women's experiences and dilemmas regarding balance.

In this book, I use the term *manager* because most of the people I have studied and worked with have been managers. But the ideas here apply to others, such as professionals and entrepreneurs, who share characteristics with managers. Moreover, because the problem of imbalance is pervasive in our society, these ideas may apply outside the corporate and managerial world. For example, the novelist Graham Greene was once asked how it felt to be a great success. He replied sadly that, although his writing *career* had been successful, he did not feel that his *life* had been successful. Likewise, fire fighters, artists, accountants, community volunteers, everyone who regards work as a priority, can be haunted by the difficulty of maintaining life balance. My suggestions speak to all of them.

Overview of the Contents

The Introduction outlines the dimensions of the problem of imbalance, its costs for personal life and for management effectiveness, and the components of a possible solution. Chapters One, Two, and Three each describes one of the three levels of imbalance; each gives a concrete description of the phenomenon, the forces shaping it, and its consequences for the individual's well-being. The first level of imbalance, described in Chapter One, concerns the time, energy, and commitment managers give to the different areas of their lives. Chapter Two looks at the attitudes and behaviors with which managers approach all areas of their lives and describes how these contribute to excessive focus on work. Chapter Three deals with the means and the criteria by which managers gain a sense of self-esteem. Throughout these chapters, we see how these levels create the phenomenon we call imbalance. Furthermore, we see how the pursuit of self-esteem shapes both behavioral and attitudinal patterns, which in turn affect the investment of time and energy. Each of these chapters includes exercises that enable readers to assess themselves and their organizations. These assessments are used later to catalyze discussion on how to solve the imbalance problem.

In Chapter Four we turn to solutions. This chapter provides a structured opportunity for readers to think about and make choices to establish balance in their behavior, their approach to relationships, and their approach to life in general. Balance in each of these areas will be somewhat different for every individual; I focus on general processes for approaching self-exploration. These processes are conceptually tied to the nature of the problem and allow for each individual to reflect and develop in line with his or her unique needs. These processes can also guide those who are involved in diagnosing and counseling others in moving toward balance.

Chapters One through Four frame imbalance as a problem that primarily harms individual life quality and well-being. Chapter Five looks at the ways in which imbalance can hurt individual work effectiveness and create destructive organizational cultures. Chapter Six presents a process that can be used to change organizational policies, practices, and culture so that they support organization members' development toward balanced lives and create a new climate for effectiveness.

The Afterword concludes by discussing the implications of balance in the context of the future of managerial work and organizational functioning.

How to Read This Book

Writing this book has been a journey of self-exploration. I began with a great deal of interest in other people's balance problems, and as I have explored and responded to their lives, I have had to confront the balance issues in my own life. I hope that this book will take readers on a similar journey. I encourage all readers to approach this book personally and to apply its messages to their own lives. I am willing to wager that balance is an issue for every person who opens this book. Readers' interests may be primarily pragmatic or intellectual—some may counsel executives or conduct research on work and family issues. Even so, ultimately the key to enhancing our ability to learn about and improve balance in others' lives is the extent to which we address the balance in our own lives.

The exercises included throughout the book are intended to encourage self-reflection on key issues. In particular, taking time to do the exercises will make the chapters that discuss solutions more personally meaningful to each reader and will provide the raw material for working through the change processes.

Acknowledgments

Robert Kaplan and Wilfred Drath, my teammates at the Center for Creative Leadership, supported me through the genesis and early development of these ideas. Several friends and colleagues reviewed manuscripts, challenged my thinking, and generally nudged me to finish; they include Douglas Bowie, Joan Bragar, Pamela Dennis, Diane Ducat, Marilyn Paul, Linda Rodgers, Jeffrey Sarnoff, and three anonymous reviewers. Bill Hicks and Cedric Crocker at Jossey-Bass and Judith McKibben, my development editor, gave fantastic editorial and moral support. I am also thankful to the managers and organizations who were courageous enough to participate in this sometimes difficult work.

The people who have helped by being part of my life and my development over the past years include my friends, who know who they are and how important they are; my parents, Nancy and Tom Kofodimos, whose support and love have been unwavering; Barbara Metz, who encouraged me to honor myself; and Kyle Dover, who demonstrates every day what balance is all about.

Greensboro, North Carolina   JOAN KOFODIMOS
June 1993

THE AUTHOR

Joan Kofodimos is a partner in the Renaissance Group, a consulting practice focusing on human and organizational development. As a researcher, consultant, teacher, and writer, her primary interest has been exploring the link between individual growth and organizational effectiveness. This interest has led to specific projects developing senior management teams, creating high-involvement organizations, and implementing large-scale cultural change. In addition, Kofodimos counsels executives on balancing work and personal life and helps organizations create cultures and practices that are more supportive of balanced lives.

Kofodimos is an adjunct faculty member at the California School of Professional Psychology in Alameda. She also serves as an adjunct staff member of the Center for Creative Leadership, where she worked from 1982 through 1988. Kofodimos is coauthor of the book *Beyond Ambition: How Driven Managers Can Lead Better and Live Better* (1991, with R. E. Kaplan and W. H. Drath) and has written several articles about executive development, teamwork, and strategic leadership.

Kofodimos received both her B.A. degree (1979) in psychology and her M.A. degree (1979) in sociology from Stanford University, and her Ph.D. degree (1986) in organizational behavior from Yale University.

Kofodimos lives in Greensboro, North Carolina, where she is pursuing a balanced life that includes intimate partnership, good friends, travel, exercise, and spiritual development.

BALANCING
ACT

Facing the High Costs
of Imbalance in Our Lives

A recent advertisement depicts a young, smiling, confident man in a pin-striped suit walking along carrying a baby in a backpack. The caption suggests that real success comes from knowing one's priorities.

A newspaper article describing the new trend to "drop out of the rat race" tells of a woman who, "after twenty years on the New York fast track working her way through the ranks of an insurance company," quit her job and moved to Vermont, where she now works as a secretary. "No more 16-hour days. There is time for baking cookies, ice skating with her niece, even dating."[1]

A newspaper article relates tales of increasing numbers of people leaving fast-track jobs to spend more time with their families. In one story, a high-powered attorney took a rare day off to celebrate his daughter's birthday. "I remember sitting on that merry-go-round with [my daughter] thinking: 'How much is it worth giving up times like this?'" As a result, he soon quit his job to take another, at a 75 percent pay cut, which enabled him to spend evenings, weekends, and holidays with his family.[2]

Career counselors report an exponential increase in the number of clients who want to switch their fast-track lives to slower paced careers providing more "personal fulfillment" and "quality of life."[3]

1

These anecdotes, taken from popular magazines and newspapers, are signs of the times. They may strike a chord for managers whose lives center around demanding jobs and careers. These tales capture a common fantasy of a different life, one with more time to smell the flowers, more fulfillment in family, friends, spiritual or religious pursuits, health and fitness, and other aspects of a well-rounded life apart from work. A number of popular surveys and polls reflect managers' increasing inclination to question the value of a life focused on work. A poll in the *Wall Street Journal* showed that over half of five hundred male executives would accept pay cuts of up to 25 percent in order to have more family or personal time.[4] Yankelovich Clancy Shulman, a research firm that conducts an annual survey on American values and life-styles, reported in 1990 that both men and women are beginning to "reassess the trade-offs between work and family."[5] This trend is also evident in Roper poll findings regarding Americans' views on work and leisure. In 1991 the Roper organization announced a "waning work ethic," after finding that only 30 percent of respondents saw work as the "important thing" in their lives—a record low, down 6 points from 1989 and 18 points from 1980. In contrast, the 1991 percentage of respondents describing leisure as the "important thing" was 36 percent, and the perception that work and leisure were equally important rose to an all-time high of 24 percent, up 9 points since 1980.[6]

In part, this increased interest in life balance is a result of demographic shifts. The baby boom generation, which now represents a sizable chunk of the managerial population, is reaching mid-life, a time of adult development that is typically characterized by a quest for meaning and a reassessment of the life structure that an individual has spent earlier years developing.[7] The mid-life transition is precipitated by the realization of our own mortality, which leads us to question how we want to spend our precious remaining time on earth. Thus people at mid-life are prone to critically assess whether their choices and actions reflect what is most deeply important to them. Another important demographic shift is the entry of numbers of women into management and professional ranks. Women are traditionally more interested than men in integrating work into active personal lives, but the organizational system of values and rewards in which they must work is based on the over-arching commitment to work.

In part, these changing values and needs may represent a historical pendulum swing away from the emphasis on ambition, achievement, and financial success prevalent in the 1980s. In that decade, according to historians, the gradual loss of leisure that had been occurring in the American middle class over the prior two decades reached its most extreme point.[8] It may be that participants in the work-and-success frenzy of the 1980s found that the single-minded pursuit of success did not deliver the fulfillment it promised.[9]

Although so many managers complain that work has taken over their lives and express the wish that things be different, the stories about giving up investment banking to restore old farm-houses or to sail around the world do not represent the norm. More typical are managers who do nothing, or at best struggle to change how they invest their time and energy, with only mixed success.[10]

The form of this struggle varies from individual to individual. One person feels overweight and out of shape, repeatedly vowing to begin a fitness program but unable to commit to the effort or find the time in an overfilled schedule. Another, recovering from a divorce, copes with the loneliness by spending every waking hour working. Yet another feels pressure when forced to decide between meeting an important deadline and attending a child's birthday party. A manager with a family wishes she had more time to spend with them: she loves her husband and children, and at the same time feels estranged from them. A single executive wishes he had more time to build a social life or indulge in his hobbies. All these people share the feeling that work has taken over their lives, that their lives are out of balance.

What lies beneath this apparent inability or reluctance to change the imbalance between work and personal life? How does it happen that people who have demonstrated the talent, commitment, and willpower to climb in an organization's hierarchy and to run multimillion-dollar operations seem unable to develop the skills they need to take charge of their own lives? Why do they see their life structure as controlled by external pressures? When these people set business objectives, they will turn the world upside down to achieve them, but they meekly blame external pressures for their unsatisfying lives. The result is a discrepancy between what managers say they value and the values they demonstrate by their behavior.

The Discrepancy Between Values and Behavior

I received evidence of the discrepancy between values and behavior when I visited a graduate seminar at the Tuck School of Management at Dartmouth University in the spring of 1991. The seminar professor, James Walsh, and I asked the group the following two questions. You might want to respond to these questions as you read on.

1. Assign percentages according to the *importance* of each of the following areas in your life (they should total 100 percent):
    Work   _____
    Family (or intimate relationship)   _____
    Leisure   _____
    Community   _____
    Religion   _____
2. Assign percentages according to the amount of *time and energy* you devote to each of the following areas in your life (they should total 100 percent):
    Work   _____
    Family (or intimate relationship)   _____
    Leisure   _____
    Community   _____
    Religion   _____

The average scores for the twelve participants in the seminar were as follows:

	Importance	*Time and Energy*
Work	30 percent	62 percent
Family	40 percent	15 percent
Leisure	20 percent	20 percent
Community	6 percent	2 percent
Religion	4 percent	1 percent

These students felt that family or intimate relationships was the most important element in their lives, but their behavior was inconsistent with that value. Work got a disproportionate share of their time and energy relative to its stated importance.

The students responded to the survey results with expressions of frustration: "Yes, but is it possible to have it all? That's unrealistic!" "I can't let up on work—the pressures are so intense!" "I need to work hard now to build my credentials for the future!" "Companies require long hours for career advancement!" "I'm just doing this for my family's benefit!" The energy that goes into justifying the focus on work suggests that powerful forces are involved, and, indeed, they are. Imbalance is a deeply motivated phenomenon, which accounts for its imperviousness to change and for the profound ambivalence toward change that managers experience.

The Origins of Imbalance

We will discuss all of these arguments in time, but here we will address just one: executives' and managers' (and management students') perceptions that organizational pressures are to blame for their overwhelming focus on work. Organizational values, norms, and reward systems do indeed contribute by setting in motion a spiral of imbalance in which an executive or manager devotes increasing amounts of time and energy to work, then experiences an increasing pressure to work and greater rewards from work, and then increasingly neglects personal life. But the organization is not the only source of pressure. Internal forces—our own needs, wants, and drives—also get in the way of balance. The lopsided allocation of time and energy is merely a consequence, or symptom, of deeper issues.

Executives and managers—males in particular—tend to take a particular approach to living, which we can describe as a striving for mastery and an avoidance of intimacy. *Striving for mastery* is characterized by emphasis on task accomplishment; by perception of other people as work roles, human assets, or instruments for getting the work done; and by reliance on rational analysis in making decisions. *Avoidance of intimacy* is characterized by a relative lack of empathy and compassion, inattention to our own and others' feelings, reluctance to experience and express vulnerability and self-doubt, and discomfort in being playful and spontaneous. This pattern of preferred and avoided attitudes and behaviors leads some managers and executives to be more comfortable with workplace culture and norms, which tend to value mastery-oriented attitudes and behaviors, than with the typical settings and demands of personal life, which place relatively greater value on intimacy-oriented attitudes and behaviors.

Furthermore, under the striving for mastery and the avoidance of intimacy lie needs that have to do with identity and self-worth. Managers and executives who strive for mastery and avoid intimacy do so because they find the inner experience of mastery rewarding and supportive of their self-esteem, while the experience of intimacy is threatening to self-esteem. For example, a sales executive may spend weeks chasing a lucrative contract because he enjoys the feelings of self-worth that come from winning the contract. But he may not spend the same time and energy in pursuing a personal relationship because when he becomes close to a potential partner he feels vulnerable and insecure. Such an individual has learned to gain esteem by creating and pursuing an idealized self-image. This image portrays a person who is masterful, who has attained mastery. The image is idealized because it is fictional; it hides unwelcome and unacknowledged aspects of the individual's real self. In contrast, the qualities and experiences of intimacy are inconsistent with the idealized image and, even worse, threaten to reveal those unwelcome aspects of the self. For example, the sales executive described above would not like to see himself described as vulnerable and insecure; this is not part of his self-image. It is, however, a real part of him, which is evoked by intimacy but hidden by mastery. His self-esteem is linked not to aspects of himself that come to the surface through intimate relationships, but to those aspects that are manifested through mastery—confidence, aggressiveness, and perseverance. Thus, he experiences his work as the primary setting for, and mastery as the primary mechanism for, personal growth and the development of self-esteem.

In sum, the discomfort managers and executives experience as imbalance between work and personal life actually results from the interplay among three phenomena: the focus of time, energy, and commitment on work; the dominance of a mastery-oriented and intimacy-avoiding approach to all spheres of life; and the creation and attempt to live up to an idealized image of self.

The striving for mastery and the association of mastery with self-esteem begin early in life. Most males and some females in Western society are rewarded by authority figures, such as parents and teachers, for achievement, competence, goal orientation, and confidence. They learn that they will get praise and approval by demonstrating those qualities rather than by developing capabilities for empathy, compassion, playfulness, and spirituality. However, within each person is not only a rational, confident, masterful side, but also an emotional, childlike, intimate side, which does not go away simply because we wish it gone. Therefore, being masterful often involves suppressing aspects of the self that are inconsistent with the masterful image. Thus, we sometimes avoid intimacy and focus on work, where we can safely experience our sense of mastery.

As we will see, organizational values and rewards encourage both the focus of time and energy on work and the striving for mastery and avoidance of intimacy. Mastery-oriented qualities—such as ambition, confidence, power, aggressiveness, independence, and optimism—are generally seen as contributing to a person's effectiveness. In contrast, intimacy-oriented qualities—such as asking for help, expressing feelings and doubts, being playful and spontaneous, and demonstrating empathy and compassion—are seen as getting in the way and thus are devalued and discouraged. Furthermore, organizational processes foster self-idealization by equating self-worth with upward mobility and by defining competence and performance in terms of universally applied lists of managerial "strengths" and "weaknesses."

The Consequences of Imbalance

Unfortunately, in the long term, the drive for mastery carries costs in terms of executives' and managers' effectiveness. The excessive focus on work can lead to life crises that belatedly force people to scale back their level of commitment to work. Managers and executives who strive for mastery and avoid intimacy often demonstrate flawed management and leadership behavior patterns, including inappropriate attempts to control, harsh responses to others' mistakes, reluctance to seek help or advice, resistance to critical feedback, and failure to praise or support direct reports. In addition, more general costs to the organization are likely to ensue from these peoples' high stress levels and associated health care needs.

Although society has cast an indulgent eye toward "workaholism," as imbalance is commonly called, there is increasing recognition that the addiction to work is as harmful to life quality and work effectiveness as the abuse of other substances. The widely held assumption that a person must be one-dimensional and driven in order to excel is a myth that enables work addicts to justify their behavior even when it is destructive to themselves and others.

The Challenge of Seeking Balance

If imbalance is indeed so deep-rooted and so harmful, what can be done to address it? Solving the problem will require that individuals change their approach to living and that organizations review and critique their values, norms, and practices.

As we come to grips with the depth and complexity of imbalance, it will become clear that it is indeed possible to have a fulfilling personal life and also, ultimately, long-lasting career success. We will see, however, that a manager or executive who has found balance defines success somewhat differently than one who is leading an imbalanced life. In fact, we will see that the mastery-driven person's definition of success is part of the phenomenon of imbalance. Managers and executives who maintain a balanced approach to work, family, friendships, play, and self are more likely to be happy in life and effective in their work roles.

Creating balance does not involve following a standard recipe for devoting equal amounts of time and energy to work and to personal life. Rather, balance involves finding the allocation of time and energy that fits your values and needs, making conscious choices about how to structure your life, and integrating inner needs and outer demands. Balance involves the ability to express, and experience rewards from expressing, both masterful and intimate sides of one's self. And it involves honoring and living by your deepest personal qualities, values, and goals.

By the same token, organizations that support balance will do more than develop family-friendly policies. They will redefine the notion of effective performance to incorporate a wide range of individual talents, contributions, and styles, and they will redefine the notion of career to respect a range of individual aspirations and definitions of success.

one

The Time/Energy Imbalance: Putting Work Above All Else

An imbalance between time and energy happens when managers and executives focus the lion's share of their time, energy, and commitment on work. It is manifested in their staying at the office into the evening, traveling frequently, entertaining clients over dinner, and taking full briefcases home for the weekend. Even when they are not "working," work often occupies these peoples' minds. While they sit at the family dinner table, their thoughts may be miles away, back in the plant or the conference room. When they go on vacation with their families, they may drag along an extra suitcase full of books, magazines, and memos related to the job.

Michael Bono*, vice president of research and development in a large manufacturing company, had a long history of unsuccessfully fighting the time/energy imbalance. He recalled that in graduate school, with a wife and new baby, he had "worked all the hours that you could imagine for three years." He continued this pace in his first job, but "with only two weeks of vacation—and I never used all of it—I burned myself out after a couple of years." He changed companies as a result, only to find that his new bosses "did the same thing to me again, dumped on me every major problem they had. I was working all hours." He put up with it, though, because these were high-visibility problems, and the reputation he gained by

*The names of the people mentioned in this book have been changed to protect their privacy.

10

solving them propelled him from team leader to vice-president in just seven years. Here, he thought, he could slow down a bit. As he explained: "I certainly plan to spend more time with Cathy and the kids than I have over the last few years. I've wanted to do it more, but I've had to establish myself at the corporate level. I've moved up kind of quickly. It's just turned out that way, but I like to take advantage of opportunities. Now the business needs me so badly that I have the power to set limits on what I'll do."

A few weeks after he said this, another area was added to Bono's responsibilities and he canceled a family trip in order to attend to them. Even though Bono had resolved, once more, to "set limits," his desire to be responsive to organizational demands and the promise of further rewards overpowered his good intentions.

Managers and executives in every type of organization voice the same refrain: the work is never done. Those from one organization voiced opinions such as the following: "This job will drive you to imbalance, if you let it." "There's so doggone much to do." "I know when it's time to stop working because I fall asleep on my desk." "The pace of this firm is crazy. You can be totally busy from a breakfast meeting to a dinner meeting." People in management roles are given as much challenge and responsibility as they can take. The task of operating an organization is never complete in the way that performing a technical task might be. Many respond to their jobs with marathon efforts to get everything in order, rather than putting an uncompleted project aside, admitting it won't get finished that night, and going home.

The Life Spheres Assessment (Exercise 1.1) is designed to help you evaluate the time/energy imbalance in your own life. Filling it out now will prepare you to apply information about contributing factors, given in the next section, to your own situation.

Factors Contributing to the Time/Energy Imbalance

Several forces contribute to the pressure to overwork, including new workplace technology that makes it easier to bring work home, global interactions that require twenty-four-hour communications, and competitive pressures brought on by today's economy. Elements that combine with these pressures to skew life structures

Exercise 1.1. Life Spheres Assessment.

Using the following rating scale, respond to each statement:

1 = very dissatisfied
2 = slightly dissatisfied
3 = neutral
4 = slightly satisfied
5 = very satisfied

Then, for each category, calculate your average score. A higher score indicates a higher level of satisfaction. Finally, try to identify the major areas of satisfaction and dissatisfaction in each category.

Work

1	2	3	4	5	1. I feel challenged by my work.
1	2	3	4	5	2. I have good relationships with my co-workers.
1	2	3	4	5	3. I have special skills and talents that enable me to excel at my work.
1	2	3	4	5	4. I have fun at work.
1	2	3	4	5	5. I contribute to society through my work.
1	2	3	4	5	6. I get recognition and respect at work.
1	2	3	4	5	7. My job is a good fit with my abilities and values.

(Total) _____ divided by 7 = _____ (average score for work and career).

What is going particularly well in my work and career? _____

What particularly needs improving in my work and career? _____

Family and intimate relationships

1	2	3	4	5	1.	My family and I participate in activities, hobbies, and interests together.
1	2	3	4	5	2.	My family loves, appreciates, and supports me.
1	2	3	4	5	3.	I have a lot in common with my spouse/intimate other.
1	2	3	4	5	4.	I have good relationships with my family members.
1	2	3	4	5	5.	My family and I have fun together.
1	2	3	4	5	6.	I talk with my family about what is going on in my life and theirs.
1	2	3	4	5	7.	I have a satisfying sexual relationship with my spouse/intimate other.

(Total) _____ divided by 7 = _____ (average score for family and intimate relationships).

What is going particularly well in my family and intimate relationships? _____

What particularly needs improving in my family and intimate relationships? _____

Friendship and social life

1	2	3	4	5	1.	I have friends outside of work.
1	2	3	4	5	2.	I enjoy my social life.
1	2	3	4	5	3.	My friends and I talk about the important wishes and concerns in our lives and provide support for one another.
1	2	3	4	5	4.	My friends and I do enjoyable things together.
1	2	3	4	5	5.	I see my friends as often as I'd like to.

(Total) _____ divided by 5 = _____ (average score for friendship and social life).

What is going particularly well in my friendship and social life? _____

What particularly needs improving in my friendship and social life? _____

Exercise 1.1. Life Spheres Assessment, Cont'd.

Community involvement

1. I contribute and give back to my community.   1 2 3 4 5
2. I pay attention to local and national politics.   1 2 3 4 5
3. I am an involved and informed citizen.   1 2 3 4 5
4. I contribute what I can (time, money, and so forth) to causes that matter to me.   1 2 3 4 5

(Total) _____ divided by 4 = _____ (average score for community involvement).

What is going particularly well in my community involvement? _____

What particularly needs improving in my community involvement? _____

Physical self

1. I eat healthy nutritional food in moderation.   1 2 3 4 5
2. I participate in a regular exercise program.   1 2 3 4 5
3. I get adequate rest.   1 2 3 4 5
4. I do not abuse drugs, tobacco, or alcohol.   1 2 3 4 5
5. I am comfortable with, and like, my body.   1 2 3 4 5

(Total) _____ divided by 5 = _____ (average score for physical self).

What is going particularly well with my physical well-being? _____

What particularly needs improving with my physical well-being? _____

Mental, emotional, and spiritual self

1	2	3	4	5	1.	I take time every day to rest, relax, and take care of myself.
1	2	3	4	5	2.	I have a special hobby or pursuit that I enjoy and make time for regularly.
1	2	3	4	5	3.	I attend to my spiritual development.
1	2	3	4	5	4.	I am living my life in accordance with my values.
1	2	3	4	5	5.	I find opportunities for intellectual or cultural stimulation outside work.
1	2	3	4	5	6.	I actively seek to understand and improve my emotional well-being.

(Total) _____ divided by 6 = _____ (average score for mental, emotional, and spiritual self).

What is going particularly well with my mental, emotional, and spiritual self? _____

What particularly needs improving with my mental, emotional, and spiritual self? _____

include career rewards, Western society's work ethic, role polarization, overload, and love of work.

Workplace Technology

Michael Bono had taken to wearing a beeper in recent years, and he used a car phone and had a fax machine at home. As is typical of today's manager, he had difficulty getting far enough from work to forget about it. Thanks to explosive advances in workplace technology, managers and executives are constantly besieged. They get electronic messages on their home computers—or are expected to call in for their voice mail on Saturdays and Sundays. Commuters can now establish offices in their cars, fully equipped with phone, fax, and personal computer. Most resort hotels have fax machines, and when executives and managers go on vacation, their secretaries and bosses routinely ask for the hotel's fax number, in case "something comes up."

And the increasing popularity of cellular telephones and beepers makes it possible to contact a manager or executive anywhere, anytime. Recently, National Public Radio's "Morning Edition" news program carried a story involving a man who took his cellular phone on a fishing trip! The commentator interpreted this as the ultimate allegory for the modern loss of true leisure time, noting that fishing used to be the holiday of choice for people who wanted to get far away from civilization, where nobody could find them.

Global Business Interactions

When we combine the new opportunities and pressures created by technological advances with the globalization of business, the result is a twenty-four-hour workday. To communicate with colleagues in Asia, Europe, or elsewhere, executives and managers must keep extended hours. Michael Bono had colleagues in Japan. To talk with them, he had to telephone them at nine o'clock in the evening, and would often stay on the line until eleven. People in leadership roles are always slightly on edge because a telephone call or fax message could come along at any moment, from anywhere in the world, requiring a response that is thoughtful and prepared.

Competitive Pressures

Today's increasingly competitive economy is another factor that encourages executives and managers to focus on work. As more and more companies downsize in the attempt to streamline operations, the survivors must pick up the extra work. And because cutbacks might continue or resume at any moment, the survivors live in fear. They see their co-workers as rivals for scarce resources. They feel they are under continual scrutiny for evidence of their value to the company. They worry that if they turn their attention away from work—to take a vacation or to attend to a family problem—they will lose ground, a competitor will advance onto their turf, their commitment will be questioned, they will return to a pink slip and a cleaned-out office.

Such fears are not completely groundless. As economic pressures have increased for American business, job security has become a thing of the past. Executives' and managers' jobs are at risk and must be earned over and over by excellent performance and constant proof of dedication to the company's success. This message is conveyed daily to employees by means of changing policies and practices, such as one Fortune 100 company's recent elimination of pension benefits, a cost-cutting move justified by estimates that executives' and managers' tenure with the company will average less than five years.

Organizational Evaluation and Rewards

Organizations—the people surrounding the executive and the manager at work; the work processes they have evolved; the systems of rewards, measurements, development, and succession; and the norms of behavior they have implicitly agreed to—influence managers and executives to focus a great deal of energy on work, and they are rewarded for doing so, especially during the early years of their careers. A young manager's experiences and achievements are often scrutinized by organizational decision makers to determine whether or not he or she is to be considered "high potential."[1]

A manager in the early stages of his or her career may therefore justify extra-hard work by saying it is a temporary necessity that will result in advancement to a secure position where he or she can relax a bit. But the demands continue. Acquiescence to long hours, frequent travel, and repeated relocation is treated as proof of loyalty and dedication throughout the person's career. As one senior manager commented, "In my company, there is an emphasis on hours. More hours is better. It shows you're committed." She described the political game in her organization: "If your boss gets in at six-thirty in the morning, you come in at six-fifteen. Then, you make sure to walk by his office or send him E-mail, so he knows you're there." Similarly, an article in *Fortune* magazine notes that "companies view willingness to get up and go as a sign of dedication. Consequently, travel assignments are often received as badges of merit."[2]

Large and geographically dispersed organizations, such as today's typical corporation, have traditionally relied on geographic transfers as a means of development and career advancement. Reluctance to accept such transfers is thought to reflect a lack of commitment. Said a partner at a consulting firm, "The norms here have been to give your all. If you set boundaries, your commitment is questioned." Managers and executives are aware of such unstated norms. As one said, "In this company, you can refuse one transfer but not two." After two, the transfer and promotion opportunities simply stop coming, and, worse yet, the individual is labeled a nonplayer in the fast-track organizational game.

Some managers, executives, and observers of management life claim that the pressure to accept geographic transfers is becoming a thing of the past. Others say the expectation that executives and managers put such work requirements first is alive and well, although it may be increasingly unacceptable to voice this explicitly. Behind closed doors or in senior executives' minds, the willingness to move for the job may still affect who is classified as high potential, who receives the developmental opportunities requiring a geographic move, and who ultimately reaches the top echelons.[3]

For example, one manager refused a promotion opportunity that would have required a move to another state because he did not want to uproot his high-school-aged children. His co-workers generally saw this as the major cause of his subsequent relegation to a dead-end job. Said one, "Charlie turned the general manager job down because of his family situation. His family liked where they were. He had never put his family first before. He was too honest to hide that, even if it meant getting into trouble with top management." Did Charlie get into trouble? Said the company's chief executive officer, "Charlie has potential in terms of his intelligence and organizational capability—but *maybe not in terms of his commitment.*"

Exercise 1.2 allows you to look at your organization's culture in terms of the extent to which it encourages an excessive focus on work. We will return to the results of this assessment in Chapter Six when we discuss how to change organizations so they support balance.

Emphasis on Work in Western Culture

Organizational reward systems are not the only source of pressure to focus on work. The norms and institutions of our society as a whole contribute significantly. The value traditionally placed on work has been conveyed through socialization to the male role, but achievement-oriented women in work environments shaped by these values are affected as well.

Some members of the academic community hold the mainstream social sciences partially responsible for perpetuating our culture's overarching value of and admiration for work. One researcher argues that those who study organizations tend to treat "the tendency to overperform in occupations and underperform in all other roles" as normal.[4] For example, one group of researchers conducted studies founded on the assumption that work is the overwhelming and "central fact of life," the fact that determines all other facts of our lives.[5]

What are the effects of this value? The executives and managers studied by one group of researchers "upheld as an ideal lifestyle one in which professional and private life were separate and independent . . . [but, in fact,] while private life concerns and thoughts rarely interfered with work, job concerns did pervade fam-

Exercise 1.2. Organizational Expectations Regarding Time, Energy, and Commitment.

Put a plus sign (+) next to items on the following list that are positively valued in your organization or that represent desirable qualities in managers. Put a minus sign (–) next to items that are negatively valued in your organization or that represent undesirable qualities in managers.

You may want to respond to the items twice, once regarding what you think is expected of you by others in the organization, and once regarding what you expect of others in the organization.

Another way to respond to these items is to ask yourself which items best describe a person who does well in this organization.

Imbalanced commitment (focus on work)

—— Maintaining a "full plate"—a heavy, stressful workload

—— Consistently spending long hours at the office

—— Traveling to and from work destinations on weekends

—— Giving work obligations priority over personal obligations

Balanced commitment (focus on work and personal life)

—— Talking about personal life at work

—— Refusing for personal reasons transfers or promotions requiring geographical moves

—— Starting a family—becoming pregnant or adopting a child

—— Going home during the workday to attend to personal responsibilities, such as a sick child

——— Preserving a family structure whose demands are minimal (for example, a male having a traditional spouse or a female remaining single or childless)

——— Accepting work-related phone calls at home on evenings or weekends

——— Doing work at home regularly

——— Accepting frequent transfers and promotions that require geographical moves

——— Taking an extended parental leave

——— Setting limits on hours spent at work

——— Using alternate work designs, such as flextime and flexplace

——— Taking your full vacation allotment

——— Preserving a family structure that demands commitment (for example, dual careers, children)

Do the pluses and minuses reveal any patterns? What does this signify about prevailing norms in your organization regarding the investment of time and energy in work?

What similarities and differences do you find in what is expected of you and what you expect of others? To what extent have you been a carrier of organizational norms regarding the investment of time and energy in work?

ily and leisure lives."[6] It is more acceptable for professional life to intrude on personal life than for the reverse influence to occur. Personal life thus can become, with society's blessings, a peripheral area on which the door can and should be closed.

The value placed on work at a societal level has a long history. During the Renaissance, the prevailing view, as expressed by thinkers such as Leonardo da Vinci, was that through working we become more divine, more like God.[7] Then, in the New World, "one of the most important underpinnings of American culture" emerged.[8] This new paradigm was the Protestant work ethic: "Men have no reason to expect to be saved in idleness, or to go to heaven in a way of doing nothing. . . . It is required of every man that he should devote himself to [work], which implies that he should give up himself to it, all his affairs, and all his temporal enjoyments."[9]

According to the Protestant work ethic, work is the only virtuous form of activity. Through work we serve God and do penance for our innate sinfulness. Perhaps even today we believe, deep down, that we can reach salvation by devoting our body and soul to our work.

Even today, many of the executives, managers, and professionals with whom I work seem to accept the pervasive organizational and social assumptions that work is the primary priority in life and that working hard is the most virtuous of pursuits. A corporate leader's colleagues implicitly support the work ethic by respecting, valuing, and encouraging work-driven behavior and attitudes. For example, a co-worker of one executive said admiringly, "I'd call Roger on Friday night and say, 'We've got to work this weekend.' I'd even call him on vacation. He never complained." Another co-worker said of the same executive, "Roger Wood is the hardest-working guy I've ever seen, very impressive. I don't know how he does it. I wish I had his energy. He does an unbelievable amount of work. Works till six, comes in on Saturday, works at home. He's the kind of guy who comes home from a business trip at five P.M. and comes here and does two hours of work."

Management experts and gurus also argue that excellence requires a one-dimensional focus on work. For example, one popular management bible of recent years states: "We have found that the majority of passionate activists . . . have given up family vacation, Little League games, birthday dinners, evenings, weekends, and lunch hours, gardening, reading, movies, and most other pastimes. . . . We are frequently asked if it is possible to have it all—a full and satisfying personal life and a full and satisfying hard-working professional one. Our answer is: no. The price of excellence is time, attention, and focus.[10] This quotation was used by another pair of writers, the social critics Anne Wilson Schaef and Diane Fassel, to support their point that the "obsession with work is promoted as desirable in the excellent company."[11]

Polarization of Work and Family Roles

Another factor contributing to the time/energy imbalance is the very life structure many male executives and managers adopt as part of their acceptance of the dominance of the work role. Most of the senior male managers with whom I have worked are married, and the bulk of them have traditional families. Their wives are often full-time homemakers and mothers, though they may be civically or socially active. Or they may have jobs with circumscribed demands, such as teaching school. Many of these women had challenging careers of their own at one time, which they gave up or scaled back as their husbands' work went into high gear.

Whether or not male executives' and managers' wives are employed outside the home, they are usually in charge of child rearing and home responsibilities. They take the role of supporting their husbands' focus on work and adjusting their families' lives to their husbands' careers. This role allows male executives and managers to make decisions, in favor of work priorities, that have implications for their families—such as working long hours, accepting transfers, traveling frequently, and thinking about work while at home. Says one such manager, "My home life is happy and stable, which gives me the security to spend energy on organizational problems. My wife is interested in my job. She's supportive of my travel, and she moves and adjusts easily."

The traditional corporate wife plays a role in contributing to the male executive's or manager's career. In addition to running home life so that her husband can focus on work, she plays an important social role at events that occur "outside the business day

but hardly outside the business boundaries."[12] In some organizations, the stability of an executive's or a manager's family life is a
factor in promotion decisions.

The corporate wife has been described as an unpaid employee of the company because of the services and support she provides for her manager-husband. This situation has been described
as a "two-person single career," in which the wife's support of her
husband's job enhances his commitment to work and benefits the
organization.[13] The boss of one manager, George Kelly, said while
describing George's strengths and weaknesses, "His wife has nothing to do with the business. It's an embarrassment to him. She's a
nice sharp young lady, but she won't go to conventions and
dinners."

Not surprisingly, ambitious, successful, career-oriented men
have been found to be more happily married and more successful
in their jobs when they have a traditional family arrangement. In
1970, a study of marital happiness and its relationship to husbands'
and wives' primary orientation, career or family, found that the
unhappiest couples were those in which the husbands were primarily career oriented and the wives were career oriented as well as
family oriented. In other words, if the husband is primarily career
oriented, the marriage is more likely to be happy if the wife is
primarily family oriented.[14]

In the more than two decades that have passed since that
study was conducted, social roles and expectations may have
changed, but organizational pressures have not decreased. Career-
focused executives and managers still benefit greatly by having a
spouse who can handle all their personal responsibilities. For example, geographic transfer is still a primary vehicle for career advancement. Many male executives and managers in my studies
moved their families every few years for new jobs and saw doing so
as essential to their career progress. Not having a second career to
relocate makes this easier. In addition, because an executive or manager is expected to jump into a new job smoothly and at full speed,
a wife is typically responsible for managing the family's transition
from their old house, schools, and community to the new ones. The
energy required to manage a geographically mobile family can thus
limit the wife's alternatives to a traditional role. It is difficult to

pursue a continuous career while juggling family responsibilities and frequent relocation. And in the case of international transfers, some governments actually forbid the spouse of an expatriate to be employed.

The role of the corporate wife thus affects the male executive or manager's career progress and is at the same time circumscribed by the demands of that progress. Although the traditional male-female division of responsibilities frees the male executive or manager to focus on professional achievement, it also limits both partners to narrow, separate roles that allow the male to become detached, even alienated, from the family. I refer to this pair of traditional roles as "polarized" because they lie at opposite ends of the work-family spectrum.

Women managers, too, experience role polarization of a sort. Another group of researchers found that, among the female managers they studied, the most common strategy for dealing with balance was to put work first: "With few exceptions, the seventy-six female executives we interviewed made the decision that a number of savvy insiders consider to be a milestone in their successful careers—the 'priority decision' to put their career first and squeeze in whatever else in life they can around it."[15] This decision often entailed remaining childless, and sometimes even remaining single and uninvolved in intimate relationships.

Multirole Overload

Of course, not all executives' and managers' lives are characterized by role polarization. An increasing number of male and female managers are taking on multiple life roles, which leads to its own form of time/energy imbalance. It is now often a financial necessity for both adult partners in a nuclear family to hold paying jobs outside the home; thus, family responsibilities must be shared to a greater degree than they traditionally have been. In the modern family, it is not realistic or affordable to assign one spouse responsibility for breadwinning and the other spouse responsibility for home life.

Even when financial necessity is not the issue, many men and women—especially in younger age groups—prefer nontraditional family structures and roles for a number of reasons. Peoples' views of what constitutes a family have diversified to include such variations as married or unmarried dual-career couples, with or without children. In these families, the ideal is a fairly equal partnership, with both people sharing work and household duties. In addition to such partnerships, many men and women spend part or all of their adult years single, with or without children, and must handle both work and home responsibilities.

The problem of multirole overload is most apparent with women. On the one hand, women with families, even women who are career-oriented, often end up with much of the implicit responsibility for parenting, maintaining the marital relationship, and managing the home. On the other hand, they also experience extra pressure from work. Female executives and managers feel that their organizations are scrutinizing them particularly closely for signs that they cannot be relied on in senior positions because their personal lives might take precedence over work demands.[16] If these women try to maintain both career and personal life as priorities, they must constantly juggle and trade off conflicting priority activities. Thus, for women, the presence of a family provokes a kind of time and energy imbalance in which they are constantly busy trying to fulfill multiple roles and responsibilities, constantly experiencing pressure to be doing and working, even though the activity occurs in many life spheres.

But men in dual-career families also experience multirole overload. I recently participated in a study of life-style pressures facing consultants in a professional firm. Their jobs were extremely demanding in terms of hours and travel, and both males and females, single and married, expressed concern and dissatisfaction. Surprisingly, the dimension along which there was the biggest difference in degree of dissatisfaction with life-style demands was not male versus female, but rather the dimension of single- versus dual-career married male. In other words, married males whose wives did not work outside the home were much less bothered by the workload pressures of their jobs and the impact of these pressures on their personal lives than were married males whose wives did work outside the home. The dual-career married males experienced multirole overload similar to what dual-career females experience, and they found it highly stressful.

Love of Work

One simple reason executives and managers tend to focus their energy on work is that they like working. This sometimes only becomes clear when a choice is forced between a successful career and a satisfying personal life. One manager, whose overarching dedication to work led to the breakup of his marriage, said, "I don't want to get into another marriage-type relationship in the foresee-able future. I know I spend a lot of time working and I don't think I'm going to change, and I know it's difficult for a lot of people to live with. If I do get into a serious relationship they'll have to be interested in what I do because they'll have to live with it as well as with me."

The truth of the matter, then, is that hard work is not only a response to organizational pressures. Managers and executives often work hard because they love their work. As one manager said, "Work is fun and should be fun." Another said, "I get a kick from this. I can even burn up because I'm too intense. Doing this work is like being on heroin. It's a big adrenalin rush. Every time, it has to be bigger. The time I worked five months without a single day off is at the forefront of exciting things I've done. Like a triathlon. You love it, but it's painful."

Exercise 1.3 lists a number of symptoms of time/energy im-balance. Filling it out will give you a sense of the extent to which you are at risk for some of the consequences we are about to discuss.

Spiraling Toward Crisis: Consequences of the Time/Energy Imbalance

All of the pressures we have reviewed can contribute to an imbal-ance, with work receiving increasing amounts of energy and com-mitment, and personal life receiving decreasing amounts.

If an executive or manager does accept the implicit contract, focusing on work in return for life on the fast track, he or she is likely to reap the rewards—praise, respect, power, money, visible

Exercise 1.3. Symptoms of Time and Energy Imbalance.

Place a check mark next to the items that describe you.

_____ I bring work home on the weekends.

_____ I continue working after my co-workers have quit and gone home.

_____ I put more thought into my work than I do into my personal life relationships.

_____ I eat on the run.

_____ I don't have enough time to stay on a consistent exercise program.

_____ I get an adrenalin "high" from dealing with pressures and challenges at work.

_____ I'm more diplomatic with co-workers than I am with family members.

_____ I find myself thinking about work while I am engaged in leisure activities.

_____ I prefer working to engaging in leisure activities.

_____ I keep promising my family that I will cut down on working, but I don't do so.

_____ I get more recognition and respect at work than I do at home.

_____ I feel overloaded by all the roles I play in my life.

_____ My organization demands a lot of work out of me.

_____ The more work I have on my plate, the more I thrive.

_____ I work harder when things are unsatisfying in my personal life.

_____ I worry about my health.

_____ I worry about the consequences for my kids of the moves we've made and my long hours.

_____ By and large, my worklife is more exciting than my personal life.

_____ I feel it's my responsibility to provide for my family, even if it means long hours.

_____ I don't have too much in common with other members of my family.

_____ I don't spend much time in conversations and interactions with family and friends.

_____ My family has adjusted to the pressures of my work.

_____ I like it when my hard work is recognized by an increase in responsibility.

_____ I feel good in my outside life because of my work position and status.

What proportion of the above items did you check? When you look at the items you checked, what is the message you get? Does it tell you your time and energy are out of balance?

achievements. In turn, these rewards and the promise of more to come provide an incentive to spend even more energy working. And, with advancement and increasing responsibility, the pressures only mount.

Deterioration of Personal Relationships and Outside Interests

More energy put into work implies less energy available for other areas, such as marriage, children, friendships, or outside interests. Researchers have found, for example, that many successful executives and managers are more career oriented and less family oriented than their less successful colleagues. Managers focused on work life turn their attention away from their families; the family's needs are given low priority as job and workplace become increasingly central. Such managers tend to lose touch with other aspects of life as well. It is no surprise that when managers' occupational demands increase, their marital and life satisfaction decrease.[17]

Thus, the time/energy imbalance feeds on itself: work dominates the individual's time and energy, neglected personal relationships become increasingly unsatisfying, and career rewards may become especially appealing by contrast. In fact, the organization may promise benefits that are missing from personal life, such as recognition and approval. Soon the executive or manager is trapped in a vicious circle: he or she turns more and more to work for gratification, and as the investment in work versus personal relationships becomes increasingly lopsided, the two areas provide increasingly discrepant levels of "payoff" in terms of affirmation and satisfaction. Managers and executives eventually choose to stay away from intimate others because they have forgotten how to interact at a personal level with those others, and they feel threatened by the prospect of facing discomfort and even rejection when they do try to engage in such interaction.[18]

Some executives and managers may blame their long work hours on a bad marriage, as did Dean Humbold after his divorce: "One reason I got involved in a lot of community activities," he said, "was that I got a lot of positive feedback from them. The reason I spent so much time outside the home was that I felt my time was valued and my input rewarded, and I didn't feel that at home." But his ex-wife saw it differently. According to her, Humbold's inattentiveness to his family was itself a major source of their marital difficulties. She recalled that he had always made his work his top priority. When they were first married and he was in graduate school, he spent Thanksgiving Day in the library. According to her, his increasing absence after a recent promotion brought their marriage difficulties to the surface: "He really wanted this job," she said. "When he got it, his investment outside the office became so small. He'd schedule time with us for concerts and plays, then call at the last minute to say, 'Sorry, I have a retirement party to go to.'" She went on to say that Humbold did not recognize the contribution of his own absence to the family tensions that developed: "Eventually I no longer relied on him to be around. I had to go ahead and plan events without him in the picture. But when I did that, he'd feel excluded and would get angry at me and the kids."

The manager's or executive's behavior can contribute to tension as well. After giving his or her best to work, the person may return home too drained to give more to the family. Further, after having spent the day being composed, in control, and in charge, the person might see home as an outlet for venting suppressed frustrations from the day, or a place where it is safe to relax the self-monitoring and diplomatic behavior required at work. As one successful manager admitted, "I put pressure on my family. I expect high achievement from them. That's okay. But I'm more abrupt, less polished with them, don't take the time or thought with them that I do with people at work. Sometimes I wish I would have said or done things differently. I'm more impatient with them than I am with the people who work for me."

As personal life becomes more impoverished, hard work can become an escape from, or even a substitute for, an unhappy personal life.[19] A plant manager in charge of a twenty-four-hour-a-day operation, who had recently separated from his wife and was living in a shoebox apartment, found Saturday nights home alone so depressing that he would spend from eight o'clock Saturday evening until eight o'clock Sunday morning at the plant, catching up on mail and supervising the graveyard shift—in order to "stay in touch with the shop floor folks."

The nature of the leadership role, with its social and recreational aspects, can make it easy for the executive or manager to use the workplace as a primary source of relationships and leisure, to such an extent that the workplace can come to replace an outside personal life. This option is especially appealing when personal life is characterized by tension, conflict, and alienation. Playing golf with clients, discussing projects with colleagues over drinks, or attending meetings in exotic locations may satisfy desires for affiliation, adventure, or varied activity and provide the illusion of a rich personal life. One writer discusses the phenomenon of "travelholism": Its victims may be seduced by the thrill of being on the go, staying in luxurious hotels, and eating lavish meals—or they may be seeking to avoid problems at home.[20]

Similarly, as the workplace becomes the primary source of personal relationships, sexual attraction may develop among people who work together closely on projects, resulting in office romances. One manager explained why his romance with a co-worker was more fulfilling than his crumbled marriage: "People I have a good relationship with are interested in what I do, and they like the same things as I do. I've realized that I'm not willing to do without shared interests and values. I want to be able to come home from a trip and talk about what happened and have it be understood."

Denial and Justification

Even as work increasingly takes over managers' and executives' lives, they may deny that it is happening or that it is creating problems. Although many of these people see a growing imbalance in their lives as a sore spot or cause for regret, they tend to deny the extent of deterioration in their personal lives, even when those around them see cause for concern. They may defensively assert that their personal lives are just fine—then they own up to their concerns and doubts. "There are no negatives in my life," said one, "but I get a growing feeling that I missed developing a closer relationship with my children. . . . Now those years are gone." One manager was approached, before his eventual divorce, by a colleague who was concerned about him. He replied, "There's nothing wrong with my personal life! I'm just never home." Meanwhile, another co-worker said, "I hope he's happy from a family standpoint. He gives too much to the job. It would be horrible if he were to lose something personally. I've talked with him about this. He's never expressed concern. He missed his kid's birthday because he was out of town, but he didn't show a lot of remorse. It was just a fact of life."

Some managers and executives who deny imbalance insist they do attend to their families and circumscribe their hours at work—a claim with which their friends and family disagree. A personal friend of Michael Bono's (who, as we saw earlier, claimed to have set limits on his dedication to work) told us, "As Michael's gone up the ladder, he's tended to assimilate himself into his work to the exclusion of everything else. He has little time in his life for anything but the company. I hardly ever see him socially anymore. I don't know what he does for relaxation. He's quit gardening, he's left our jazz band. I worry about him."

The very nature of the imbalance can inhibit awareness of its consequences for personal life. If we attend mainly to professional life, if we have other "important" things to worry about, then it is easy to see what is happening in our personal life. Yet we must wonder whether there is more to the blindness—a desire, perhaps, not to see what is happening in personal life, a fear of seeing.

When executives and managers do acknowledge the imbalance, they may justify it in terms of the need to provide for their families, put children through school, and so on. However, while they may reassure themselves that they achieved their career success for the sake of their families, the truth is usually that they did it because they *wanted* to do it.[21] Similarly, executives and managers may justify their focus on work by claiming that it is temporary and that they will stop after the current project deadline or next promotion. But there is always another deadline or promotion, and the focus on work continues.

Crisis

Whether or not executives and managers acknowledge the problems that result from imbalance in their personal lives, the effects tend to accumulate. Tension is likely in a family when one spouse devotes all his or her energy to work. Those supportive families who free the executive or manager to focus on work by taking care of home responsibilities may not continue to be so happy as the imbalance grows. Four hundred seventy-six wives of top executives reported to a *Wall Street Journal*/Gallup poll that they were not happy that business dominated their husbands' lives. The most unhappy women in this group felt that their husbands took much more from the marriage than they put into it.[22]

As the manager or executive becomes increasingly absent from home and as family members' rewards from the relationship decrease, they may begin to withdraw their support. One manager describes a simmering family situation created by a severe work/family imbalance: "Since I made the decision to throw my career into high gear, my wife couldn't understand why I didn't get equal joy from the kids and working around the house. My wife and I are having a lot of tension over my career."

This manager is luckier than many because he sees the tension and it is not too late to address the problems in his marriage. But such a situation may be the precursor to an eruption of a full-blown family crisis. Because of justification and denial, the unease may not be glimpsed until the problems have become dramatic. Indeed, many executives and managers seem so focused on work that they are blinded to problems occurring in their personal lives, as was an executive named Matt:

> [Everyone talked about how] we were the golden couple, how our marriage was so terrific, and I was buying that. . . . [Then my wife told me she thought our marriage was rotten.] That was the beginning of it. . . . I began to take her seriously when she was too depressed to get out of bed in the mornings. . . . It came as a shock to me that [my wife] questioned me, questioned her life. I thought I had that pretty well under control. The thing I learned is that you don't have a marriage and sort of put it away in a cabinet—"Now, that's taken care of." See, I think that's the marital model we grew up with: you get married and put that behind you, and get on with the important

part of life, which is building the career. You have
enough other things to worry about, your job and how
much money you're making, and you put the marriage in the cabinet because it's more comfortable not
to worry about it, and you polish it once a year on
your anniversary because it's unsettling to have to
think, gosh, you're in a relationship that might break
up tomorrow. [23]

By putting his marriage out of his awareness—"in the cabinet"—
Matt made it and its problems invisible until a crisis forced him to
look. Perhaps it would have been threatening for Matt to see his
marriage in such bad shape and his wife so unhappy; that would
have required him to admit his contribution to the problem and
might have provoked guilt feelings. It might have challenged his
self-image as a "family man" and evoked the worry that his organization would look askance at a manager with personal problems.
It might have been disturbing to see that he was hurting the people
he loved. It might have led him to feel incompetent or inadequate,
a failure as a husband.

A number of managers and executives I studied made statements similar to this one: "I was married for twenty years, had four
kids, then divorced. I'm sure my ex would say my job came before
her." A broken marriage was only one of several kinds of crises that
these managers reported and that they came to see as direct consequences of their career-driven behavior. For example, one described
the harmful effects on his children of the frequent geographic
moves the family made for his career: "This was a devastating experience, the worst thing that ever happened to me. The effects of
a transfer on my oldest son—he developed emotional problems."
Another manager talked about the heart attack he suffered at the age
of thirty-eight, which he attributed to his stress-ridden life-style.

Traumatic events had a profound impact on these people.
Perhaps this was because the events placed at risk, or took away
entirely, some aspects of personal life that they previously had
valued but taken for granted, such as a stable marriage, happy children, or their own physical health. Consequently, the managers and
executives realized that their families and their own well-being re-

quired energy and care. They questioned the priorities and values by which they had been living and came to a new realization of the importance of the nonwork spheres of their lives. They placed limits on the job commitment that had overwhelmed all else, newly seeing work as only one element of a healthy rounded life. Said the manager quoted above, who went through a divorce after twenty years of marriage: "It was earth-shattering, sobering, the most devastating experience in my life. Now I take the other side less for granted, and put more energy into it." Said another, "People who have severe family problems approach risk differently. They're more conscious of what's happening in their lives." Yet another said, "Tragedies have matured me greatly. I learned the importance of family and quality relationships."

A management consultant sums up the process leading to crisis and reassessment:

> The way you make it in this organization is to work ten or twelve hours a day, travel a lot, not see your family. Your husband or wife is saying to you, "Hey, we're getting kind of strained here." You're feeling a pull between your personal and your professional life. You've always been programmed to believe that the reason you're doing all this is for them. But by the time you get that you're not happy, you've missed life and your kids are going to college and you realize it and you begin to feel some sadness about it. . . . Sometimes there's a precipitating event outside. Your husband or wife says, "Hey, we've got serious problems. If we don't get some help, I'm leaving." Kids you've been working hard for wind up going off on drugs. You kind of do a number on yourself at that point: "Maybe I was wrong. I didn't spend enough time with them." In retrospect, you look at the whole trip you've been on.

Thus, executives and managers may deny imbalance simply because they do not want to have to do anything about it. If we truly face the imbalance and its potential consequences, we may realize that it is necessary to reevaluate our life structure, give up some things, maybe even reconsider the costs versus the benefits of career success. Ultimately, then, managers and executives may be reluctant to change their life structures because they fear losing the rewards that work has provided.

Reassessment

Managers and executives who have experienced crises, and who consequently have re-sorted their priorities and commitments, have had to renounce some of their ambition and disinvest in their careers in order to begin the work of repairing their personal lives. The following statements come from people who made the decision to climb off the fast track and leave their organizations: "I was having personal problems at home and I didn't think they were as bad as they were. . . . My wife said, 'You've got a kid going to hell in a handbasket.' The psychiatrist said, 'Go home and get your son under control.' I decided that the best thing for myself and the company was to go home and deal with the kid. I didn't have a job—we went on savings. But that's turned around. He's in military school right now, an honor student. It was the right decision to leave the company."

Said another, "We have four children and we'd made four moves in five years. But before the last move, one of our daughters was diagnosed as mentally retarded. That meant we had to be more selective about where to move so she had the chance to develop. I was asked to move to Europe, but turned it down. We may have had to stay put with our daughter for three to seven years. So I left that company and found another one where I could stay in this city for the next twenty-five years."

A former advertising executive relates how he came to terms with a crisis: "I fought and struggled to achieve [my career goals]. . . . I had no family life of any quality, and I had no personal life. . . . I kept trying harder and harder to achieve the impossible . . . until it made me sick and I had a heart attack. My illness caused me to come to my senses. I realized I wasn't doing anything that I believed in. I stopped trying to impress myself and others and went in search of what was right for me. . . . Resigned to a life of genteel poverty and obscurity, I moved to Montana. . . . I followed my nose and it led me to things I was interested in.[24]

A few managers and executives learn from others' crises. One woman I interviewed recalled that one day a highly respected and hard-working senior executive in her organization announced his impending retirement. The organization threw a big retirement party, with testimonials and mementos. But the day after the party that man had been forgotten. His name never again crossed the lips of anyone in the company. When that happened, the manager telling the story realized the transience of her own relationship with the company: "Organizations don't give lasting intrinsic value to your being—only people do." Since then, she has taken great pains to preserve a many-dimensional life, including time with her husband and children, a month of vacation every year, regular exercise, and active church involvement.

Resistance to Change

The example above of a manager transforming her approach to life is uncommon. Reassessing our lives means change, and it is natural to resist change. The prospect of change evokes fear of losing activities and relationships that have become meaningful to both life and identity. Ultimately, then, managers and executives are reluctant to change their life balance in conditions short of crisis because they do not want to lose their career success. They want to work, and success is important to them, so much so that they participate in the creation of imbalance while denying that they have done so.

Regardless of what we say, our behavior reveals the values by which we are actually living. At some level, we are *deciding*, whether consciously or not, how to use our energy. And our choice of where to put our energy reveals the roles that we most value and the aspects of our identities that are most central to us.[25]

To have a job that we truly enjoy is enviable, and many of us will make work a top priority at certain points in our lives. Doing so only becomes a problem when we love our work so much that it is all we want to do, even at the cost of our health and our most important relationships. Our next step is to explore what it is about the satisfaction of success in work that, for some of us, transcends the potential satisfaction of success in personal life.

two

The Mastery/Intimacy Imbalance: Finding Fulfillment Exclusively Through Work

In Chapter One we found that managers' time and energy get out of balance, with the lion's share of that time and energy becoming focused on work. This occurs partly because of organizational and societal pressures and rewards. The consequence is a spiraling imbalance, as time and energy spent on work increase along with damage to personal life. Managers often deny this dynamic until a crisis explodes in their lives. We also saw how managers themselves contribute to this situation by accepting organizational demands and choosing to commit the bulk of their time and energy to work and very little to their personal life.

The foregoing discussion, however, begs a crucial question. People, commitments, and interests in personal life also exert pressures and promise rewards for the manager's or executive's time. Why are work pressures and rewards more compelling than those originating in personal life? Why do managers and executives pursue the rewards of career success in ways that preclude the rewards of personal life success? There must be something about working and having a successful career that is extremely psychologically compelling, more so than loving and having a successful personal life.

In this chapter we will explore a phenomenon I call the mastery/intimacy imbalance, which underlies and reinforces the spiraling focus of time and energy on work and the neglect of personal life. This mastery/intimacy imbalance helps explain why work success is so satisfying for these managers and executives.

The existence of a split, a polarity, between two modes of experience, two ways of relating to life and the world, here called intimacy and mastery, has been observed by many writers. These two modes have been described as "the two greatest yearnings in human experience. . . . One of these might be called the yearning to be included, to be a part of, close to, joined with, to be held, admitted, accompanied. The other might be called the yearning to be independent or autonomous, to experience one's distinctness, the self-chosenness of one's directions, one's individual integrity."[1] In addition to *mastery* and *intimacy*, this polarity has been framed in such terms as *agency* and *communion, autonomy* and *interdependence*, and *instrumental* and *affective*.[2] These polarities are characterized by certain patterns of attitude, behavior, and underlying drive. The mastery/intimacy imbalance refers to a way of being in the world that both emphasizes mastery and shuts out intimacy.

The Drive for Mastery

The managers and executives I studied take an approach to both work and personal life that I will call "mastery oriented," which is geared toward the goal of experiencing mastery. The concept of mastery has been recognized by researchers for half a century as a basic and universal human need. Mastery, most broadly defined, is the experience of developing and exercising one's abilities and powers. Attaining mastery is an important means by which individuals clarify their identity, enhance their self-esteem, and feel fulfillment, pleasure, and joy.[3] For example, a person who stands upright on water skis for the first time experiences the pleasure of mastery. So does the person who successfully presents a proposal for an ad campaign to an enthusiastic client.

Mastery involves both a process, or mode of functioning, and a goal, or desired outcome. For executives and managers, mastery can become the only satisfying mode of experience and the only desired goal.

Characteristics of the Mastery-Oriented Approach

We will examine the key characteristics of the mastery-oriented approach to living through the example of Jim Wallace, age forty-eight and head of corporate engineering at a large manufacturing company. He has a wife, to whom he has been married since they were in college together, and three children, aged twenty-two, eighteen, and fifteen.

As you note how the elements of the drive for mastery play out in Jim's personal life, keep in mind that not all executives and managers display each of these qualities in exactly the same way that Jim does. There is considerable individual latitude in the way people adapt their lives to the drive for mastery.

- *Emphasis on logic, intellect, and rationality.* Jim has a Ph.D. in electrical engineering. He began his career with no intention of becoming a manager, but was promoted from his original bench position into a succession of management positions owing to his technical, intellectual, and project management capabilities. Jim continues to rely on these capabilities and finds it useful to approach problems in his life and managerial work just as he approached the scientific problems of graduate school and the technical problems of his engineering jobs—by exhaustively collecting objective information and painstakingly analyzing it.
- *Concern with people's task performance.* Jim looks at people as additional problem-solving resources, to be utilized for task accomplishment. He expects them to behave accordingly—to perform the task correctly and to respond rationally to his directives. Thus, his children serve as assistants on his many home renovation projects. He treats himself as a resource, as well; for example, he describes himself in relation to his children as an "information bank."
- *High standards for others.* Jim expects others around him—especially his family—to demonstrate excellence, to live up to his high standards. He is frequently thinking about how to spur his children to higher and higher performance and achievement. When he listens to them playing their musical instruments or

looks at the homework projects they are working on, he gives them his critical feedback.

- *High standards for self.* Jim expects a lot from himself as well. He wants to do everything "really really well, better than anyone else would do it," as a co-worker said. He prepared long and hard for a presentation to his management, saying, "I want this to be a stellar performance." This approach is not limited to a few special events: Jim prepares this hard to excel in everything he undertakes.

- *Desire to be in charge.* Jim likes to run things and is clearly in charge in his family. When he becomes involved in community activities, it is usually in a leadership capacity. He was head of his church's fund-raising committee, for instance.

- *Aggressive and action oriented.* Jim is extremely motivated by the urge to reach closure, to see results. Jim's wife comments that his primary contribution to their marriage is this action orientation: "He supplies the income, he decides what needs to be done, and he gets it done."

- *Valuing of individualism and autonomy.* Jim likes to work on projects himself. He likes the feeling of thinking through the entire process and coming to closure entirely on his own, without having to collaborate or negotiate. Correspondingly, his few hobbies are solitary ones—restoring an old sports car, puttering in the garden. Jim's political views reflect his belief in self-reliance and the importance of individuals taking responsibility for themselves.

- *Confident demeanor.* Jim's wife says, "He's not wishy washy in the least! He's confident and methodical, and not afraid to let you know where he stands." Others say Jim appears to be extremely comfortable and secure with himself.

- *Preference for activity and productivity.* Jim always likes to be busy and productive. When his last job was not challenging enough, he was bored. At family parties, Jim is the organizer. Similarly, after they built a new house, he worked long hours redoing the garden. Even Jim's pleasure reading is intended to be productive, as most of it is directly related to work. His bedside table holds copies of the latest best-selling business texts and recent issues of business magazines.

• *Serious, adult approach to life and work.* Jim takes himself, his responsibilities, and his life seriously. He wants to "do what's right." He has a strong sense of duty, and describes himself as good at "making myself do things I don't like to do."

The mastery-oriented approach to living is so ingrained in people raised in Western Culture that the foregoing description of Jim Wallace may seem normal and typical—which it is for male managers. However, there is another way of being in the world that is less normal and typical for such male managers but equally important: the intimacy-oriented approach.

Characteristics of the Intimacy-Oriented Approach

The mode of experience that contrasts most directly with the drive for mastery is the intimacy-oriented approach. This approach involves seeking connectedness with others and also with one's own inner self. Key characteristics of the intimacy-oriented approach include the following:

> An emphasis on one's own and others' feelings
> Concern with what people need and want
> Tolerance for one's own and others' weaknesses
> A desire to collaborate and be interdependent with others
> An emphasis on a rewarding and satisfying process of accomplishing things
> An appreciation for connection and deep interaction with others
> The desire to express emotion and reveal one's vulnerabilities and doubts
> A preference for leisure and contemplation
> A playful exuberant approach to life and work

A person striving for intimacy would receive pleasure and personal gratification from having a close and revealing conversation with a new friend, in which each of them shared important and personal information about their values and goals for their lives. Such a person would receive gratification from coming up with a strategy for reorganizing his or her department's work, in order to alleviate the unhappiness several direct reports were feeling about their current job assignments. Such a person would prefer doing a project collaboratively and would enthusiastically share credit and influence in return for the pleasure of teamwork. Furthermore, an objectively good end product would be of less interest to such a person than a satisfying process of working together to achieve it.

The Avoidance of Intimacy

The intimacy-oriented approach is, by definition, completely opposite to the mastery-oriented approach along every dimension. Clearly, then, to the extent that managers and executives approach the world with the mastery perspective, they do not use the intimacy-oriented approach. I continue to be struck by the almost total absence of the intimacy-oriented approach among the managers and executives I studied, such as Jim Wallace, in a range of situations and areas of their lives. Other researchers, too, have commented that male managers tend not to use an intimate mode of relating to the world.[4] In fact, some, such as Jim, seem to be actively uncomfortable with intimacy. For example, Jim mistrusted feelings and regarded emotion as a sign of immaturity.

At this point, it may help to reflect on the extent to which the drive for mastery and avoidance of intimacy characterizes your life. Exercise 2.1 provides an opportunity to assess your approach to living along these dimensions. Once you have an idea of the extent to which your approach to various areas of life leans toward the mastery- or intimacy-oriented side of the continuum, you may want to reflect on how this approach to living has helped you, and how it has gotten in your way. As with the other exercises, we will return to this one when we move to the question of personal development in Chapter Four.

The drive for mastery and avoidance of intimacy is especially noticeable in male managers, not surprisingly because it is consistent with the traditional male role, in its emphasis on rationality, power, and emotional control. There is a body of evidence to suggest that this lopsided focus does not characterize women, that in fact women's development involves integration of mastery and in-

Exercise 2.1. Checklist of Mastery- and Intimacy-Oriented Characteristics.

Think about the various spheres of your life. Assess your approach on each of the poles shown below, according to the following scale:

1 = use the mastery-oriented approach in most situations
2 = use the mastery-oriented approach somewhat more than the intimacy-oriented approach
3 = use both approaches about equally
4 = use the intimacy-oriented approach somewhat more than the mastery-oriented approach
5 = use the intimacy-oriented approach in most situations

Mastery-oriented characteristics   *Intimacy-oriented characteristics*

Emphasis on logic, intellect, and rationality   Emphasis on own and others' feelings
1   2   3   4   5

Concern with people's task performance   Concern with people's needs and wants
1   2   3   4   5

High standards for others   Tolerance of others' weaknesses
1   2   3   4   5

High standards for self   Tolerance for own weaknesses
1   2   3   4   5

Desire to be in charge   Desire to collaborate and be interdependent
1   2   3   4   5

Aggressive and action-oriented

1　2　3　　　4　5　Emphasis on rewarding and satisfying process

Value individualism and autonomy

1　2　3　　　4　5　Value connection, deep interaction with others

Confident demeanor

1　2　3　　　4　5　Express emotion, reveal vulnerability and doubt

Preference for activity and productivity

1　2　3　　　4　5　Preference for leisure and contemplation

Serious adult approach to life and work

1　2　3　　　4　5　Playful exuberant approach to life and work

What patterns do you see? What similarities and differences are there between your approaches to work and personal life?

What have been the benefits of this approach in your work? In your personal life?

What have been the costs of this approach in your work? In your personal life?

timacy.[5] However, a group of researchers studying female executives found that "executive women are more like executive men than they are different in terms of their goals, motives, personalities, and behavior."[6] These researchers found that executive women possessed such mastery-oriented qualities as self-confidence, dominance, ability to define and attain goals, self-discipline, rationality, intellectual ability, and even-temperedness. We can only speculate on how to reconcile these seemingly contradictory findings. Perhaps, although the striving for mastery and avoidance of intimacy are associated with male socialization, women are also affected when they occupy managerial roles in organizations shaped by men's strivings.

Organizational Forces Supporting
the Mastery/Intimacy Imbalance

One thing males and females in leadership positions have in common is their experience in work organizations. Not only do organizations reward a manager or executive for focusing energy on work, as we saw in the last chapter; they also shape and reinforce the drive for mastery and avoidance of intimacy. First, there is a self-selection process that brings to the organization mastery-oriented people who are motivated by the prospect of becoming managers. The drive for mastery provides the impetus that, in combination with talent, leads them to seek high positions. Then, they are rewarded and promoted because their qualities fit the accepted mastery-oriented requirements of the managerial or executive role. For example, the drive for mastery, and associated qualities such as intellect, technical knowledge, and planning and problem-solving ability, is linked to such demands as setting goals and standards, mobilizing large groups of people, and exercising power and influence in the service of organizational objectives. Then, once mastery-oriented people are placed in these roles, those desired qualities are further strengthened by organizational culture, norms, measurements, evaluations, and reward systems.

By contrast, intimacy-oriented qualities—such as emotional depth, sensitivity, caring for others, and self-awareness—are seen as irrelevant, even as creating impediments to work. This message is conveyed to managers and executives through several channels, including their own direct reports. Said a direct report of Roger Wood, "I like that he shows confidence. It makes me feel comfortable. If he showed doubt, it would make me question the course of action we were taking."

The suppression of intimacy-oriented qualities also serves a purpose in shaping a conscious self that is in tune with perceived demands of the work and one's own success. Uncomfortable feelings and thoughts would conflict with the manager's or executive's conscious attitude of confidence and enthusiasm about organizational life. For example, compassion and empathy would get in the way of the joy of competition. Loneliness and guilt would get in the way of putting personal life aside in the devotion to career success.[7]

Thus combining the drive for mastery with avoidance of intimacy allows managers and executives to remain detached from uncomfortable feelings and focused on the positive. This positive focus is extolled by many management writers, who describe how successful executives and managers minimize or overlook their failures and weaknesses, maintain an optimistic and positive attitude, and focus confidently on their strengths.[8] Nonetheless, although these qualities may indeed be associated with organizational standards of success, there are often hidden costs to be paid in terms of managers' and executives' personal development and well-being.

Organizations vary in the extent to which they encourage mastery and discourage intimacy. We can use Exercise 2.2 to get a sense of how our own organizations operate along this dimension. After you complete this exercise, you may want to reflect on the consequences of your organization's culture for the quality of your life in the organization. When we talk about changing our organizations, in Chapter Six, we will come back to the results of this assessment.

Consequences of Striving for Mastery and Avoidance of Intimacy

Although striving for mastery and avoidance of intimacy are reinforced by organizations, and although in many respects this way of approaching life is productive and functional, it also holds a number of consequences for a manager's or executive's well-being.

Exercise 2.2. Organizational Climate for Mastery and Intimacy.

Which of these characteristics are demonstrated by managers and executives in your organization?

1. Choose one item in each horizontal row that characterizes the "typical" manager's approach. Put a T next to that item.

2. Choose one item in each horizontal row that characterizes the "best," most effective, or highest potential managers' approach. Put a B next to that item.

Mastery-related characteristics

___ Emphasis on logic, intellect, and rationality

___ Concern with people's task performance

___ High standards for others

___ High standards for self

___ Desire to be in charge

___ Aggressive and action-oriented

___ Value individualism and autonomy

___ Confident demeanor

___ Preference for activity and productivity

___ Serious adult approach to life and work

Intimacy-related characteristics

___ Emphasis on own and others' feelings

___ Concern with people's needs and wants

___ Tolerance for others' weaknesses

___ Tolerance for one's own weaknesses

___ Desire to collaborate and be interdependent

___ Emphasis on rewarding and satisfying process

___ Value connection, deep interaction with others

___ Express emotion, reveal vulnerability and doubt

___ Preference for leisure and contemplation

___ Playful exuberant approach to life and work

In which columns do the characteristics of "typical" and "best" managers tend to cluster? What does this suggest about the valued and predominant leadership/management profile in your organization?

Source: Balancing Act, by Joan Kofodimos. Copyright © 1993 by Jossey-Bass Publishers. Permission to reproduce and distribute material, with © notice visible, is hereby granted. If material is to be used in a compilation that is for profit, please contact the publisher for permission.

- *Energy focused on work.* The striving for mastery and avoidance of intimacy can add to the forces encouraging managers and executives to focus their energy on work. Because work involves developing and exercising skills and capacities, it is a primary source of mastery. In contrast, other life areas and activities, such as family or romantic life with all its unpredictability and emotion, are less reliable sources of mastery. Thus, the mastery-driven person may commit increasing amounts of time and energy to work, which is more likely to yield the experience of mastery.

- *Personal life experienced as mundane.* The discrepancy between the ability of personal life and work life to satisfy the drive for mastery explains why personal life may seem mundane compared to the excitement of work. Dean Humbold said, after his divorce, that he considered his work a "calling." He added, "I feel I'm doing the right thing in spending my time, energy, and emotion on work. I'm doing something worthwhile, for the greatest public good. . . . consistent with my Christian values. What I do at work is interesting and important. It's what I enjoy. I value growth in the sense of learning, doing what I'm capable of. It doesn't have to be related to business, necessarily. It just so happens that it usually is."

    Compared to this view of work as a higher calling, the chores and routines of personal life can appear humdrum. When executives' or managers' co-workers look upon them with admiration and respect, the familiarity of their intimates can be a comedown. As one manager said, "Everyone at the office tells you how super you are. Then, when you get home, there's a woman with wrinkles who knows all your faults. If she keeps pointing them out, it creates friction." When a person is accustomed to wielding power and influence on the job, it is frustrating to feel powerless at home. "I can make a multibillion-dollar decision at work, but when I get home I can't get my teenage son to mow the lawn," said Jim Wallace. What is interesting here is how these managers define what is rewarding to them: A woman at home who knows them intimately, faults and all, is not seen as loving and comforting, but as threatening or anxiety provoking. Wrinkles are unattractive, viewed not as a sign of long intimacy with one's partner but as a lack of glamour. Making a multibillion-dollar decision is exciting, but the challenge of motivating a recalcitrant teenage son is not.

- *Striving for mastery in all activities.* The problem is not only that mastery-driven executives and managers focus their energy on work because that is a more likely source of mastery. It is also that, as we saw in Jim Wallace's case, executives and managers who are striving for mastery will apply that approach to all areas of their lives. Thus, even when they try to attend more to their personal lives, to put more time and energy into relationships, they may experience frustration. A person who applies the mastery-oriented approach in all areas of life will feel pressure to be productive all the time.

- *Relaxation difficult or impossible.* Jim Wallace feels uncomfortable without a lot to do and becomes more energized the heavier his work load becomes. He has a hard time relaxing and enjoying leisure. With no outlets for relieving tension, indeed with every activity a source of more tension, he is stressed a great deal of time, which places his health at risk. Jim's wife said, "He never relaxes. He makes a to-do list every day, even Sunday, and everything on that list has to get done. He never lets up on himself." Similarly, another manager spent fourteen-hour days at his job, and family members said they worried that he would "work himself into an early grave." But they worried even more that, during the small bit of time he spent at home, he would "practically kill himself" doing such projects as renovating their old house.

- *Structured, "productive" vacations.* At the same time that constant activity can create unrelieved stress, vacations are anxiety-provoking for mastery-oriented executives and managers. The thought of doing nothing, of being unproductive, is anything but relaxing. The mastery-oriented manager or executive deals with a vacation by scheduling every moment with sightseeing, golf or tennis lessons, catching up on management texts, even making business calls. Jim Wallace once had his secretary forward his mail to his vacation spot in Hawaii.

- *Competitive leisure activities.* People focused on mastery cannot just play. They need to compete and excel at everything. One manager decided to embark on a fitness program. He bought a racquetball racquet and made a date to play with a neighbor. As his wife recalled, "He came home and said, 'He was ten times better than I was,' and he never played racquetball again."

- *Frequent impatience and frustration.* Many managers and executives who seek mastery want to control the events in their environment and are frustrated when they experience constraints or circumstances out of their control. For example, when Jim Wallace had to deal with his town council over a rezoning issue, he "went crazy" with the need to attend to political considerations and with the slowness of the proceedings. When stuck in traffic, he would mutter epithets about the drivers surrounding him.

- *A constant need to control and manage others.* Mastery-oriented managers and executives try to master people, too, including family members and other intimates. For example, they may seek to control and manage family members' behavior and affairs. In this vein, Rollo May, an eminent humanistic psychologist, spoke of a captain of industry who tried to "transfer into interpersonal relationships . . . the same kind of power that had become so effective in manipulating railroad cars . . . The man of willpower, manipulating himself, did not permit himself to see why he could not manipulate others in the same way."[9] Similarly, Dean Humbold's ex-wife said, "When Dean came home from work, it was like he'd landed on Mars. It was difficult for him to shed his coat of authority. But home is where your intimate relationships are. You can't be with intimates in the same role as at the office. He'd talk to us as if we were the switchboard." The wife of another manager said, "He tells me where to turn, where to park the car. He tries to be in charge of everything."

- *Intolerance for others' weaknesses and mistakes.* Mastery-oriented managers and executives tend to be perfectionistic with those close to them. They are irked when those others lack capability, lack commitment, or make mistakes. And those others feel the pressure. Jim Wallace's eldest daughter reported, "Just because for a few years I goofed off and wasn't serious about my future, he hasn't accepted me as competent." The children of many managers I studied said of their fathers, "He wants me to be the best." Michael Bono's sons, aged seven and eight, were described as serious little boys. "Michael has impressed upon them the weight of their capabilities and the seriousness of their careers."

- *Intolerance for one's weaknesses and mistakes.* Similarly, these managers are tough on themselves. Jim Wallace is hard on himself when he violates his own "internal sense of achievement and excellence." When his performance in a recent presentation did not meet his expectations—although it was more than competent in the eyes of others—he stewed about it for days, repeatedly playing through the scenario and identifying things he could have done differently. Said his wife, "He gets disgusted with himself if he feels he's not one hundred percent perfect."

- *Task-oriented interaction with intimate others.* Mastery-oriented executives' and managers' interactions with others in their personal lives, such as their children, tend to be structured and task or goal oriented. For example, for a year, one manager spent weekends building an addition on his house, with his three children as apprentices. Another manager, who spent only a limited amount of time with his two daughters, aged eight and ten, did reserve Saturday mornings for "goal-setting sessions" with them.

  Certainly the quest for mastery has its place in the family; the family has tasks to accomplish and goals to meet, and an important aspect of raising children is to coach them in building intellectual and practical skills. Yet a fulfilling family and personal life also involves the ability to build and maintain intimate and harmonious relationships and to be sensitive to others' needs and feelings. And raising children involves playing with them and simply enjoying spontaneous childlike pleasures. Such pleasures felt uncomfortable for Jim Wallace, who was awkward with his children when they were young for this very reason. As his now grown-up children recalled, "He couldn't let go and have fun." As a result, they reported feeling intimidated and not free to be themselves.

- *Few personal friends.* Often, managers' and executives' only friends are their co-workers. Certainly it is natural for camaraderie to develop, and for friendships to form, in the setting where people spend most of their waking hours. Typically, however, these friendships are confined to intellectual exchange and interaction between work roles. Managers and executives may not even see these friends outside the workplace, except at company functions. One manager, Ed Santiago, said that working with others was the easiest way to develop close friendships with them. But the co-workers with whom he felt close did not feel that way about him; many said that they had never really gotten to know Ed personally. Santiago's wife commented, "In the office he is very much in control. He is removed from intimate emotional relationships. It's the one area where he functions superbly. He doesn't have to worry about hurting anyone's feelings. He handles superficial working relationships really well, where they don't demand deep emotional give-and-take."

The focus on workplace relationships allows us to circumvent the closeness and mutual revelation of "private" aspects of self that might be expected in a relationship outside the workplace. In a truly "intimate" friendship, friends disclose personal information about themselves, their fears and their wishes, the issues that are giving them concern; they engage in play activities together; they express any concerns they feel regarding each other's behavior or life circumstances; they even express anger to each other. These elements are not likely to characterize relationships centered in the workplace.

- *Distance in personal relationships.* Just as executives and managers carry on their "friendships" where their personal and inner lives are unknown, they also limit the intimacy of the relationships in their personal lives. For example, many male executives and managers, Jim Wallace included, refuse to talk to their wives about their work because, they claim, that is how they set boundaries on their work. But by doing so, they are also maintaining a distance, avoiding revealing themselves, and denying their partners access to an important part of them. Furthermore, they are denying their partners the opportunity to provide support and nurturance.[10] To this point, Jim's wife complains that he is emotionally guarded and does not share his feelings with her. She goes on to say that Jim is not as romantic as she would like, not good at telling her he loves her. His demeanor in the family can be stern, cold, and gruff.

- *Suppression of feelings, inner needs, and fears.* Of course, executives and managers who avoid intimacy do indeed have feelings, needs for love and nurturance, and fears of rejection and loss of esteem—but they often hide these needs and fears from themselves and others. Michael Bono says that he prefers not to reflect on his own life and feelings because "it feels like I've lifted a trapdoor with things swimming around underneath. I'd rather focus my attention on constructive things like helping mankind." By looking away from their inner lives, such managers and executives create a distance between their inner and outer selves. And by not sharing their inner lives with others, they create a distance between themselves and others.

- *Feeling rushed, overloaded, pressured by deadlines.* Managers and executives often describe themselves as feeling as if they are racing against the clock, overwhelmed by too many commitments. They demonstrate a frantic pace at work and at home. Jim Wallace said, "At work, I have to make the most of every minute." One way to interpret such compulsive activity and busy-ness is that it may be a strategy for avoiding intimacy with others and one's own inner self. According to Rollo May, "Activity [can serve] as a substitute for awareness. . . . Many people keep busy all the time as a way of covering up anxiety: their activism is a way of running from themselves. They get a pseudo and temporary sense of aliveness by being in a hurry, as though something is going on if they are but moving, and as though being busy is a proof of one's importance."[11]

- *Reluctance to ask for help.* Jim Wallace, like many other managers and executives I studied, considered it a sign of weakness to ask for help. His wife joked about his legendary unwillingness to ask strangers for directions when they were driving somewhere, even when they were hopelessly lost.

- *Unwillingness to accept input.* Jim felt "defeated" when others offered feedback or revisions to his plans and proposals. Because he was perfectionistic toward himself, he saw such input as implying inadequacy on his part.

- *Difficulty handling conflict.* By avoiding intimacy, the manager or executive ironically deprives him- or herself of the tools needed to deal with problems in personal relationships that often result from that very avoidance. In one case, resentment, aggravated by lack of communication, built up between a manager and his wife. She resented him because he was away working most of the time; he resented her because she did not support his career, and, as he said, "All she cared about was the kids." As the resentment and tension increased, they became unable to talk about problems without risking an explosion, so they simply stopped talking. Against her wishes, they moved across the country for his promotion, without discussing her concerns either before or after the fact. Neither of them had any idea how to resolve their situation. They eventually sought counseling, but, as the husband observed, "It would take an enormous amount of work to get back to a position where we have anything in common."

Using Work as a Defense Against Personal Problems

When personal life is not going well as a result of an overfocus on work, mastery-oriented managers and executives often work even harder, perhaps in part as a defense against dealing with personal crises. Some, who are experiencing events such as divorce, respond by becoming more intensely involved than usual in their work. Instead of finding opportunities to restructure their life-styles, they become vociferous in their affirmation of work and their denial of guilt or regret. Working focuses attention outside themselves, onto "safe" areas, such as future goals, productive activities, rational thoughts, and analyses. In this protective mode, work functions as "character armor . . . the arming of the personality so that it can maneuver in a threatening world."[12] In other words, work can function as a sphere in which we feel worthy because we feel skilled, competent, and masterful. It keeps us distant from others, and thus protects us from feeling vulnerable by preventing the loss of control that intimacy would bring. It gives us something firm to hold on to and gives us a justification for our behavior and our approach to the world.

perhaps our only place of "acceptance" + "success"

Addiction to Work

We have seen that work provides executives and managers with inner rewards that family and leisure do not, and, at the same time, work helps them avoid the painful dynamics present in family and leisure. The combination of the time/energy imbalance and the mastery/intimacy imbalance leads to workaholism, or addiction to work. Many executives and managers, when they hear the term, reply indignantly, "I'm not a workaholic! I could stop any time. I just don't choose to stop because I love to work!" Or, they may wear the term proudly, as a badge. This is misdirected pride, for addiction to work is "the only disease that draws applause from others, [that is] rewarded at every level of society," even though it "destroys relationships and kills people."[13] A person who works hard and loves work is not necessarily a work addict; some people work hard, love their work, and are happy that way. But work addicts, denying their addiction, as do other kinds of addicts, and arguing that they work because they enjoy it and could stop any time, will in fact work, or think about work, even when it costs them their health, well-being, and relationships with friends and family. They will think about work even during the times spent with family and leisure activities. Not working provokes anxiety and discomfort. Dean Humbold admitted, "I never feel I've done enough. When I have a backlog of stuff, I'd rather do that than have fun. I like having a lot to do! If I have work and I'm not doing it, I get anxious. If I'm not doing something useful, I feel guilty. I fear that I'm basically lazy. I get anxious if I'm not overscheduled. I feel more comfortable having too much to do. It feels horrible to waste time. I panic when I find myself with ten minutes free." Among the worries expressed by Dean's friends were, "He's like a machine!" "When will he stop?" "How much can he take before he burns out?"

Roger Wood, who was admired by his co-workers for his capacity for hard work, had a friend who worried about him: "I don't see how he keeps it up. I worry about his health. He tends to be sickly. If he goes on with the intense schedule, it strikes me he could kill himself on the job." Could he slow down? I asked. "No, it's not in his makeup."

The compulsive and addictive nature of the mastery/intimacy imbalance helps to explain why executives and managers deny imbalance until it has reached crisis proportions. It also helps to explain why they rationalize and justify their overwork, developing myriad ways of not taking responsibility for choosing to work hard, and why they claim (and believe) that they will slow down after the next crunch or after the next promotion. But there will always be just one more project or deadline, because the work-addicted person is terrified of the prospect of giving it up.

We all may experience some of the consequences I just described—energy focused on work, personal life experienced as mundane, and so on—while others may not seem to fit our personal situation. You can get a more explicit picture of the extent to which, and the ways in which, you are experiencing consequences of the mastery/intimacy imbalance by completing Exercise 2.3. Be as honest as possible. Your responses will serve as feedback to you, so take a moment to think about what your pattern of responses means and how you feel about it. We will return to the exercise in Chapter Four.

The important thing is that although there is nothing inherently unhealthy in the need for mastery, it becomes unhealthy when we make it a twenty-four-hour-a-day pursuit, pair it with an extreme avoidance of intimacy, and adhere to it even when it threatens our health and family. In the next chapter we will get to the bottom of why this happens.

main thesis here
— people don't work effectively when they have personal failures + problems
— more likely to hit the skids

Exercise 2.3. Consequences of Mastery/Intimacy Imbalance.

Place a check mark next to the items that describe you.

_____ I spend most of my time and energy working.

_____ After the excitement in my job, my personal life sometimes seems uneventful.

_____ I feel guilty when I am goofing off instead of accomplishing things, even on weekends.

_____ When I go on vacation, I schedule every moment with activities.

_____ When I play sports or games with my friends, I play to win.

_____ I get impatient when I have to wait in line or in traffic.

_____ I like to take charge and help others manage their affairs, even in my own family.

_____ I get frustrated with people when they don't live up to my standards.

_____ I get upset with myself when I make mistakes.

_____ I don't like to do things at which I'm unskilled.

_____ When I spend time with my partner or children, I like to have a goal or project to work on.

_____ Most of the people I see socially are people I have met through work.

_____ My family and friends don't always see the real me.

_____ I don't like to burden others with my doubts and worries.

_____ I often seem to be in a hurry and pressured by deadlines.

_____ I push myself too hard and exhaust myself.

_____ I take on too many projects and commitments.

_____ I prefer to do things myself rather than ask for help.

_____ I like to do things my way, and my way is often right.

_____ When things aren't going well in my personal life, I throw myself into my work.

_____ When I sense tension between myself and my spouse or partner, I prefer to avoid it.

Look back on the check marks you gave. What does the total number, and the pattern of items you checked, tell you? How do you react to seeing this self-description?

three

The Idealized Image: Trying to Be Who We Think We Are

As we have seen, managers' and executives' frustration with the balance between their personal and professional lives stems from interacting forces. Executives and managers tend to focus a great deal of their time and energy on work at the expense of their personal lives. A primary force shaping this investment of time and energy is that it serves the drive for mastery and the avoidance of intimacy. The work setting is a more reliable forum for experiencing mastery than the personal environment, so executives and managers prefer to invest their energy there. When they do turn their attention to personal life, they tend to do so with the same mastery-oriented approach they use at work, which has costs for the development and maintenance of intimate relationships and for the individual's physical health and emotional well-being.

This argument does not explain why executives and managers cannot search for mastery in a healthy way and also appreciate intimacy. Why are mastery and intimacy framed as opposing and incompatible forces? The reason, I believe, lies in the third and deepest level of imbalance: the level at which many of us carry an "idealized image" of ourselves, a picture of a type of person that we want to be and feel we should be.[1] This image emerges out of the messages we received during our upbringing and is reinforced by our ongoing environment, including the work organization. The image always incorporates a set of "shoulds": who we should be, how we should feel, and what we should want. Furthermore, we

59 *the "ideal self"*

seek to live up to this image, and our self-esteem depends on how closely we feel we are living up to it. The problem with this dynamic is that the idealized image does not match the range of dimensions of our real selves. Thus, seeking to live up to the idealized image involves not acknowledging our real selves and not respecting our real values, needs, and talents.

In this chapter we will see how pursuing the idealized image leads us to strive for mastery and avoid intimacy and to focus increasing proportions of our energy on work while neglecting our personal lives. We will examine how two sets of forces drive us to pursue the idealized image: the shaping of our character in childhood and present-day organizational values and pressures.

Childhood Origins of Self-Idealization

A key concept in the argument here is that each individual's character is shaped substantially by early formative experiences. Though the individual continues to develop throughout life, and continues to be influenced by important events and situations, childhood experiences leave an enduring mark.

Psychoanalytical theorists have investigated the ways in which the typical process of child rearing affects the child.[2] When parents bring a child into the world, they invariably hold particular desires for the child. They seek to shape the child's behavior by rewarding evidence of desired qualities with tenderness and affection and by punishing evidence of undesired qualities with anger and anxiety. That may happen in different ways. For example, children with ambitious and doting parents may be rewarded for their talents and achievements—for winning games, earning A's in school, being the best at whatever they pursue. In contrast, the children of perfectionistic and dominating parents may be criticized for not achieving highly enough or for not being popular or athletic enough.

Consequently, the child comes to learn that certain behaviors are "good" and others are "bad." More importantly, the child receives an implicit message from parents: We will love you if you are a "good" child and reject you if you are a "bad" child. As a result, children develop the belief that some aspects of themselves are "good" and that others are "bad," a situation that has been described as "conditional love."[3] Children begin to understand that love and approval are forthcoming from parents only if they become the "good" people their parents want them to be. Now, to a young child, parents are incredibly powerful; they are, in essence, the child's entire world. Children therefore adjust their behavior and expression of feelings to conform to their parents' wishes, in order to win their love. The child learns to get a sense of self-worth by being the kind of person who gains parental approval—rather than by just being the child's own self.

Although parents may consciously believe that punishing unwanted qualities and instilling new ones in this way is "for the child's own good," their underlying motive is more likely to be something else—such as their own need for the child to become a certain type of person, or their need to feel that they have been good parents. Their behavior has costs for the developing child. Because they do not love or honor the child for his or her individual qualities, because instead they may be demanding, critical, indulgent, or negligent, the child develops "a profound insecurity and vague apprehensiveness," which has been termed "basic anxiety."[4]

The parents' recognition and honoring of the child's need to be understood and respected by them is crucial to the child's development of a stable identity. But parents who provide only conditional love neglect the child's "real" self and inner feelings. Because the child's sense of security depends on the parents' love, and because the child suffers from disapproval for being "bad," he or she learns to hide personality aspects that are "bad" and reveal only those that are consistent with what the parents have defined as "good." This revealed self is what the psychoanalyst Karen Horney called the "idealized image" and what Carl Jung called the "persona."[5] Furthermore, the child shapes his or her consciousness around the revealed self, so that even the child no longer distinguishes between the image that is shown to the world and the whole self hidden inside. The specific nature of this experience varies according to the particular family, as the following examples will show.

The Golden Child

Dean Humbold grew up in a religious, middle-class, small-town home where he was the special, favored child. He usually exceeded his parents' standards for him, which were high relative to their small-town environment, but not relative to the wide world Dean came to envision himself entering. His mother recalled Dean as a good boy, "smart and ambitious." "We were so happy with him," she recalled. "He never gave us a moment's trouble."

Although he engaged in occasional youthful escapades, such as getting drunk and wrecking the family car, his parents never acknowledged these occurrences; such behavior was not part of their definition of Dean. Dean's wife, who had known him since childhood, said, "Dean's parents' expectations were that only excellence was okay. His successes were lauded. You never heard about anything else. There was not much room for doing anything wrong. . . . I don't think Dean grew up with a view that we all have pluses and minuses, that if you make a mistake you don't bury your head in the sand."

Dean's parents avoided pushing him toward specific directions or achievements, but they did expect certain moral qualities from him, such as honesty, integrity, diligence, and respect for authority—all of which he demonstrated amply. They also expected emotional temperance. They themselves never raised their voices, cried, or hugged and kissed; they never talked with Dean about personal matters. He came to internalize their moral code and to accept their wisdom: that achievements and moral rectitude were good and that expressions of emotion and intimacy were to be avoided. He sought to maintain his parents' love and approval and to avoid disappointing them by living up to their expectations of him. "He always wanted to please his father, always wanted everything he did to be perfect," recalls Dean's mother. He was involved in so many school and church activities—the yearbook, band, student government, and so on—that no time was left to play. As Dean grew up, he repeatedly gravitated to situations in which he could be "special": the youngest, the most talented, the favorite of his superiors.

Now a rising executive and pillar of his community, Dean continues to spend as much time as possible in productive structured activity. If his work does not keep him fully occupied, he finds boards of directors or local political activities in which to get involved. He still seeks to meet his parents' expectations in order to maintain the feeling of being special he had when he behaved in ways that gained their approval. He assumes that those good qualities he learned early will be admired and rewarded by the significant others in his adult life, and that if he shows the bad qualities he will face others' disappointment or rejection.

Dean feels pressure to "perform" in most situations: "I don't like to get behind in my work. I feel I haven't done a good job, [even though] ninety percent of the time no one notices. It's a fear of appearing stupid, unknowledgeable, ill-prepared in front of others. In college, at the dorm, I read the *Wall Street Journal* and the *New York Times* cover to cover before breakfast [so that I could] spend breakfast talking with a friend about world events. I enjoyed that. In my past job, my boss was very well read about everything. Once or twice he'd ask me my opinion and I felt bad that I had none. He asked because he respected my opinion, and I think he was disappointed that I didn't have an opinion." It is possible that Dean's boss was indeed disappointed, but equally possible that he simply was curious or polite, but did not care deeply whether Dean had an opinion on world events. Regardless of the truth, which we cannot know, Dean's interpretation of his boss's behavior is significant.

It appears that Dean experiences ongoing pressure to be perfect in order to fulfill his parents' hopes.[6] As long as he accepts this pressure, he will always have a shaky sense of self, because down deep he knows he cannot live up to the image of perfection instilled by his parents. This becomes even more apparent when he enters the world and is faced with his real imperfections. One descriptive term for such a person is "narcissistic." Narcissus, recall, was in love with his own image. Though in popular usage "narcissistic" denotes a person with a big ego, true narcissists do not have strong egos at all, because if they find themselves anything short of perfect they feel worthless. Thus, narcissists may appear abundantly self-confident, but they need continual external validation of their worthiness, via others' admiration, respect, and devotion.

The golden child will grow up with lofty aspirations and lofty visions to fulfill, but such a child is in danger of never really "owning" those aspirations. They were transferred to him or her by powerful parents who were seeking to fulfill their own wishes and desires through their offspring. Adults who still carry these expec-

tations are destined to forever seek to fulfill someone else's dreams
rather than their own, unless they are willing to find out what gifts
and inclinations lie inside them.

The Wounded Child

By contrast with Dean, another manager, George Kelly, grew up in
an ethnic, urban, working-class family. Dominating, critical, and
physically abusive, his mother conveyed to him her expectation that
he would become a failure, just as his weak and ineffectual father
had been. In reaction to this prediction, and out of economic need,
he worked from an early age at delivering newspapers, mowing
lawns, and doing odd jobs. "I never had a childhood," he recalls.
Others remember George as a solitary youth who was "serious and
self-contained" and "oddly dignified." His self-containment was
protective; he did not trust others and felt he could rely only on
himself.

George has spent his life trying to escape his beginnings and
prove his mother wrong about him. "Underlying all my achievement was wanting to show her I could do it," he said. Even now,
he regularly sends his mother his press clippings, but despite his
tremendous career success, he is never satisfied and continues to
push himself. "He sees everything as a test of his manhood and his
mettle," said a friend. Work is his source of self-worth as well as a
refuge from pain. When his son got into trouble at school, George
threw himself even further into his work. He cares very much about
his family and wants his children to have the youth he never had,
but he was awkward with them when they were young and spent
little time with them. It was as though, never having been a child
himself, he cannot be comfortable with children.

His children, now grown, wish their father could let go and
have fun—but he can never work hard enough to gain his mother's
approval and thus his own self-acceptance. For George, mastery
through career success represents an attempt to vindicate himself
and to gain a measure of self-esteem that will cancel out the rejection and powerlessness he still feels from his early years. In an
attempt to negate his early vulnerability, he has constructed a seemingly invulnerable and self-sufficient protective mask that allows

him to appear unhurt by lack of love and approval. His protective mask carries over into his work style, earning him a reputation as an organizational "hatchet man." He is sent into situations when someone hard as nails is needed to do whatever it takes to whip a unit into shape.

The wounded child wants to display his emerging capabilities and be admired for them, but his parents don't admire them. On the contrary, they are likely to punish him, laugh at him, or ignore him. The child spends his life searching for external validation and recognition which he needs in order to feel worthy, in order to overcome the "bad" person he was made to believe he was. He always feels inadequate, but he creates an outward self-image of egotism and callousness as a defense against feeling unloved. He has convinced himself that he does not care whether he is lovable and is no longer anxious to please. To survive, he hardens his heart.[7]

The Responsible Child

Ted Maxwell grew up in an alcoholic family. His father would come home every night from his job as a clerk in a shipping company and proceed to get drunk and pass out. Ted remembers his mother as quiet and passive, but kind and loving. She had all she could handle to keep the household together. Often Ted would find her crying. Ted, as the oldest of six children, became the one his mother leaned on. She would send him to bring his father home from the neighborhood saloon. Ted did the wash, took care of the younger kids, and kept a stiff upper lip. He learned that feeling pain was a luxury he could not afford because he had to be strong for his mother. He put on a happy face for the world and went out to become a leader. He was involved in sports and had an active social life with many friends and girlfriends. "Everyone looked up to him," recalls an old friend.

He also vowed that when he grew up he would raise his family differently. "I promised myself that because my childhood wasn't great, my kids would experience a better one." And he has done what he set out to do. His wife and children love him. On the surface, his life appears balanced. He sets aside time for family, takes vacations with his wife, and attends his sons' sports events.

But he is strained by the pressure of continually wearing the happy face. Everyone who knows him sees him as up, positive, and strong. When he lets down his guard, which he does rarely and with few people, he admits that he feels sad but doesn't like to express it because he doesn't want to "bring others down." With his friends, he is always the one who provides advice—never the one who needs advice. As one friend said, "He always has to be top dog." Ted often feels anxious, but he hides his anxiety. He worries a lot, and many of his nights are sleepless. Outwardly, as his sister puts it, "he wants as little disharmony as possible."

Because he cannot tolerate weakness in himself, he has a hard time accepting it in those who are close to him. When his wife cried over a tragedy that occurred in their town, Ted was uncomfortable. His wife says that the message she gets from Ted regarding such episodes is that "there are certain things it's not okay to feel."

The quality of Ted's life and the depth of his relationships with his intimate others suffer because of his reluctance to own up to the sad and hurt side of himself, and because of his need to remain in charge and responsible to others. He is exhausted by the self-induced pressure to be perfect and take care of others.

Ted's life quality is not all that is compromised. His managerial style is also shaped—and flawed—by his need to be in charge. Though he sees himself as a teddy bear, others see him as competitive, driven to win and succeed. In his fear of revealing any vulnerability, he affects a demeanor of bravado. In his intolerance of weakness, he is impatient with others who do not measure up to his expectations of them, and can become sarcastic and cutting.

In Ted's youth he essentially received no parenting. In many respects, he himself took the parenting role for his parents and siblings. He was not allowed to have needs of his own, and no one around him was able to give him the praise and approval he desperately wanted but could not ask for. As a result, he continues to seek approval without admitting it to himself or others, by continually pressuring himself to be perfect and in control.

As the examples of Dean Humbold, George Kelly, and Ted Maxwell demonstrate, a wide range of family circumstances can produce a person who pursues an idealized image of self. Every manager I've talked with eventually reveals a story like one of these three, often after beginning with mythical tales of an idyllic childhood. (Sometimes getting to this level of disclosure requires considerable shedding of the defense mechanisms established over the years.) What we all share, at this deep level, is the experience throughout early life of not having our real selves honored and respected and of getting rewards for being other than our real selves. The strategies we devise for coping with the pressures of parents and other authorities have a common intent: to gain self-esteem by creating and displaying an idealized image, which includes the elements we have learned are "good" (strong, rational, invulnerable) and excludes the elements we have learned are "bad" (emotional, dependent, vulnerable). Unfortunately, the consequences of these strategies live on, even after we cease to be children and think we are grown up.

Exercise 3.1 can help you to understand the origin and the nature of your own ideal image by reflecting on the messages you received during your childhood and their impact on you. It may help to allow yourself some quiet time for these recollections. After you have responded to the questions, think a moment about the impact of these messages on you and how you feel about the form of your ideal image. To what extent does it serve you well, and to what extent does it get in your way?

Consequences of Presenting an Idealized Image

Continual striving to live up to an idealized self-image holds a number of consequences. It leads us to engage in a range of protective strategies geared toward maintaining the illusion that we are our idealized images, while at the same time our day-to-day behavior manifests contradictory and destructive behaviors when unacknowledged sides of ourselves emerge. Furthermore, self-idealization also leads to striving for mastery and avoidance of intimacy, to excessive ambition, and to addiction to work. In other words, pursuing the idealized image leads to imbalance.

Illusion-Preserving Strategies

As we have seen, we seek not only to display the idealized image to the world but also to believe that we are that image.[8] We try to hide

Exercise 3.1. Ideal Image Portrait.

Family messages

Behavior and qualities my family expected from me (for example, make straight A's, always be well groomed, make lots of friends)

Activities my family encouraged (for example, sports, academics, playing a musical instrument)

Values my family taught me (for example, honesty is the best policy, children should speak only when spoken to)

What my parents wanted me to be when I grew up (for example, a businessperson, a doctor)

Memories of receiving my parents' approval

    What I did:

    What they did to show their approval:

    How I felt:

    What I learned about how to act:

Memories of receiving my parents' disapproval

    What I did:

Exercise 3.1. Ideal Image Portrait, Cont'd.

What they did to show their approval:

How I felt:

What I learned about how to act:

What I wish my parents had done for me that they didn't do

Consequences of family messages

Characteristics of the kind of person I strive to be (for example, wealthy, respected, intelligent)

How I would like others to perceive me (for example, honorable, creative, sexy)

Characteristics of the kind of person I strive not to be (for example, irresponsible, disliked, unsuccessful)

Things that really get on my nerves about others (for example, indecisive, loud and boisterous, let others walk over them) from ourselves and others those aspects of our character that we do not want to reveal, as if wishing them gone could make them vanish. But our inner reality cannot be changed by mandate; these "shadow" aspects will continue to exist and exert their influence. In times of stress or emotion our shadow will pop up, unbidden, into consciousness or behavior.

The case of Fred Morrison illustrates the effects the shadow exerts from its hiding place. At first meeting, Fred was quite impressive: ambitious, confident, self-possessed. Many co-workers thought highly of Fred and even saw him as a role model. But over time, it became clear that there was more to Fred than this heroic picture. Such seemingly inconsistent qualities as a volatile temper, self-doubt, and insensitivity emerged from time to time. Fred himself failed to acknowledge these inconsistent qualities, though there was undeniable evidence of their existence. For example, unbeknown to his family, he had dropped out of college after a year of poor performance and career indecision, ridden a motorcycle, worked in a warehouse, and drunk to excess.

As a manager, and in stark contrast to his typical steady demeanor, he occasionally threw temper tantrums and publicly humiliated his direct reports. In spite of the value he placed on integrity, he had an extramarital affair with his secretary. And sometimes he secretly still drank too much.

When others confronted him about these issues, he denied them. It was as if any chink in his idealized self-image threatened the collapse of the entire thing, as if acknowledging any of the bad qualities would render the good qualities invalid. If he could not be heroic, he must instead be scum.

Like Fred, when we pursue an ideal self-image, our self-esteem depends on our ability to convince ourselves and others that we are that ideal. But because the ideal image is an incomplete picture of our real self, our self-esteem is contingent on maintaining an illusion. Thus, we must engage in protective strategies so that we can feel and appear that we are living up to the idealized image. One such strategy is to justify our behavior. For example, Fred Morrison argued that, because of the circumstances, the affair with his secretary actually demonstrated his integrity. He explained his emotional outbursts at work as didactic techniques for teaching his direct reports critical thinking.

Another strategy for keeping up the illusion of an idealized image is to attribute evidence of our shadows to outside forces. As one manager said, "If my subordinates were more competent, I wouldn't have to get on their backs so much!" Or, we may create phony weaknesses to cover the real ones. These phony weaknesses are intended to create the illusion of humility and awareness of our shadow side while actually contributing to the construction of the ideal image. For example, one manager, when asked to describe his weaknesses, reported, "I'm bad at details." Other phony weaknesses commonly reported include being naive about politics, shy, or absentminded—qualities the manager is actually proud of. Focusing on these allows a denial of shadow-side weaknesses, such as selfish, insecure, ruthless, or angry feelings and impulses.

Yet another strategy for protecting the idealized image is to modify our feelings to correspond with how we think we should feel. For example, one manager, when asked how he felt after his wife had just walked out on him, replied, "I feel fine about it." Thus, the emphasis is not on being but on appearing.[9]

In addition to all of the above, a primary protective strategy for maintaining the illusion that we are our idealized image is a phenomenon we have seen already: the striving for mastery and avoidance of intimacy.

Compulsive Striving for Mastery and Avoiding Intimacy

Because intimacy involves reflecting inward and getting to know all aspects of our inner selves, it threatens to allow unwanted feelings from the shadow to seep through to consciousness where we must confront them. Because intimacy also involves revealing ourselves to others, it threatens to allow others to discover that shadow. Thus, if we are seeking to maintain the idealized illusion, we will avoid connecting with our inner selves, perhaps by engaging in constant outward-focused activity; and we will avoid connecting with others, perhaps by focusing our energy on nonintimate relationships, such as those centered in the workplace.

Workplace relationships are not necessarily nonintimate, but they lend themselves to being so. The workplace is a perfect setting for the illusory gratification of our idealized image. We can gain respect and admiration for our competence, authority, intellect, and achievements, while the intimate details of our selves and lives remain unknown. For example, Ed Santiago, who saw his workplace friendships as his closest and most satisfying, assumed in those relationships a demeanor of self-sufficiency, contentment, and stability. Ed's co-worker "friends" were not privy to his insecurities or fears. Though Ed's marriage was secretly falling apart, a co-worker said, "How does he really handle this big job and also keep up his family life? He's so in charge of himself. There must be times he sits and worries. He's not really open about what bothers him. He likes to give the impression nothing does bother him. I can't believe that. But he's never let his guard down with me. Ed bucks others up, not vice versa." Even an old friend said, "I was shocked when Ed and his wife separated. There was no reason to believe they didn't have a great relationship." Ed admitted, "I valued the appearance of a good marriage."

Overall, then, the combination of striving for mastery and avoiding intimacy serves as a protective strategy supporting the idealized image of self. The visible outcome of this is addiction to work: a compulsive drive for mastery and avoidance of intimacy which serves to create self-esteem through the illusion that we *are* the perfectly masterful images we present. Seemingly irrational workaholic behavior becomes understandable in light of the psychological threat posed by stopping working: the experience of mastery could be lost and self-esteem thus would be jeopardized.

Ambition

Another consequence of self-idealization is ambition. Most of the executives and managers I studied were ambitious. They wanted to move up in their organizations or in other organizations. Most wanted their responsibilities to be increased, and many wanted to receive outward recognition of that increase in responsibility in the form of compensation and other symbols of rank. They also tended to equate successful progress up a hierarchical career ladder with their own personal success and development. Thus, hierarchical position serves as a badge of our value; it mirrors the extent to which we have achieved our idealized image. Ambition reflects our desire to attain elevated hierarchical positions and thus our desire to move closer to truly becoming our idealized image.

A number of phenomena are linked with ambition in the executives and managers I studied. These phenomena have also been found to characterize executives and managers in previous research studies.[10] When we are ambitious, we tend to identify with our superiors. Our superiors represent what we want for ourselves, in terms of achievement, power, and status. They represent our idealized images. Wanting to be like our superiors, we seek to please them. For example, Michael Bono was consistently seen in a more positive light by his superiors than by his direct reports. That was because Michael was showing a more positive side of himself to bosses than to subordinates. He was more invested in being seen positively by his bosses than his direct reports because approval by his bosses was psychologically important to him. His bosses were the role models he admired and wanted to emulate, whose positions he aspired to achieve.

When we are ambitious and identify with our superiors, we may experience a sense of duty and loyalty toward our superiors and our organizations. We subordinate our internally derived wishes for ourselves to the wishes of the organization and our bosses, who have the power to help us succeed, as we did with our parents. Furthermore, we develop a value system that makes suppression of our own wishes in the service of our duty a virtue. For example, Ed Santiago said, "I can make myself do things I don't like to do and do them well." This was not painless. Santiago also described a time when he had to lay off a large number of employees in a way he disapproved of and felt was highly insensitive and irresponsible. He did so, but broke out in hives and still harbors a deep resentment toward the company.

Many of us who are ambitious are also insecure. At the same time that we want success, we fear failure. One writer described this as our "sense of the perpetually unattained."[11] If our progress upward through the organization is blocked, we experience anger or dissatisfaction. Where does this need to move up originate? Perhaps it is rooted in self-idealization and its early link to not being loved for who we are. As one writer suggested, the fantasy inherent in ambition is that if we can just get promoted far enough, "we will be able to do what we want and be loved for it; we will finally have some control over others and the world; we will finally belong and be at peace."[12] Hence, our identification with superiors: no matter what level we have reached, there is always a "someone" higher up, who has reached that place where he or she fits in, has power, and is accepted. We want to be in that place. This is a fantasy, because those above us share our insecurity and imagine yet another position above them where they dream of experiencing control and security. No matter what position or level we have attained, we may still feel insecure, on "probation," fearful that at any moment others will discover that we are frauds and impostors, even though we hide this fear beneath our confident personas.[13]

Thus, ambition and the desire to move upward originate from the interplay between our shadow-side fears and feelings of inadequacy, and the promise of alleviation of these psychic pains if we gain advancement in the organization. We fantasize that if we move into our superiors' positions we will become our idealized images and will finally be worthy. Thus, when we focus our energy and commitment on work at the expense of personal life, it is ultimately driven by the idealized images on which our self-esteem depends.

Exercise 3.2 can help you reflect on the extent to which these consequences of self-idealization are true for you. Again, this exercise is for your own insight and will be useful to the extent that you are honest with yourself. After you have responded to the items, look back on your pattern of responses. What do they tell you about how self-idealization is affecting your life?

The Organization's Contribution to Self-Idealization

In summary, our construction of and belief in an idealized self-image exert powerful influences on how we shape our life structures. Although the process of self-idealization originates in childhood, it remains powerful throughout life because social institutions, particularly work organizations, continue to encourage our attempts to live up to the idealized image. As you read the following descrip-

Exercise 3.2. Consequences of Self-Idealization.

Place a check mark next to the items that describe you.

_____ I like people to know that I have a respected position in my
organization.

_____ I like to convey a certain image of myself to others.

_____ When things go wrong, I tend to look around for the culprit.

_____ I want to move up in my organization.

_____ I sometimes demonstrate some personality traits that I don't particularly like.

_____ I have a lot of willpower, and I can control my feelings.

_____ I prefer not to introspect; I'd rather focus on action in the external
world.

_____ If my organization really valued me, they would promote me to a
higher level.

_____ I admire many of my senior managers and would like to become
more like them.

_____ I want my bosses to think highly of me.

_____ Part of my job is to carry out duties I don't particularly enjoy or
value.

_____ Sometimes I think the people above me in the organization have all
the power.

_____ Doing well in my work and career helps me feel good about myself.

---

tion of organizations' role in self-idealization, you may want to
reflect on the corresponding questions in Exercise 3.3, which allow
you to look at the extent to which your own organization's culture
promotes self-idealization. The exercise also portrays the alternative, a culture that supports self-realization. _Self-realization_ refers to
individuals' development in ways that are consistent with their true
talents, values, and visions for themselves.

If we are striving toward an idealized image of career success,
our ambition dovetails nicely with the organization's interest in
bending us to its own ends. Specifically, organizations' hierarchical
structures and the very notion of advancement play on our unconscious belief that success and promotion will allow us to approach
that idealized image for which we strive. Because we subordinate
our needs to those of the organization, because we are willing to do

Exercise 3.3. Cultural Practices Shaping Self-Idealism Versus Self-Realization.

Place a tick mark next to the statement in each horizontal row that best describes your organization's culture (either self-idealizing or self-realizing).

	Self-idealizing culture	*Self-realizing culture*
Performance standards: Employee voice/input into performance criteria	—— Work design, goals, and measurements are engineered by managers or experts. —— Changes in roles, structures, and demands are engineered by managers or experts.	—— Individuals have input into their work design, goals, and measurements. —— Individuals have input into changes in roles, structures, and demands affecting them.
Influence, efficacy, control	—— Outcomes on which individuals are measured are affected by numerous variables out of their control. —— Measures and standards are defined by managers or experts, not the individual. —— Role expectations and performance demands are changed without providing coaching and training.	—— Individuals have influence over outcomes on which they are being measured. —— Individuals are involved in the definition of measures and standards for their work. —— Individuals get coaching and training to carry out changed role expectations and demands.
Clarity of communication of performance expectations	—— Espoused performance standards differ from actual ones. —— Individuals are faced with conflicting performance expectations and standards. —— Changes in role expectations are not clearly explained to people. —— Individuals do not understand their role in supporting overall company goals and strategies.	—— Espoused performance standards are consistent with actual ones. —— There is consistency among the performance expectations or standards placed on individuals. —— Changes in role expectations are clearly explained to people. —— Individuals understand their role in supporting overall company goals and strategies.
Clarity of feedback regarding performance and potential	—— People do not receive clear, honest, and accurate feedback regarding their career future.	—— People receive clear, honest, and accurate feedback regarding their career future in the organization.

Value placed on authenticity or conformity	People do not receive clear, honest, and accurate feedback regarding current performance. Constructive disagreement with organizational policies or decisions is suppressed. Focus is on managing impressions.	People receive clear, honest, and accurate feedback regarding current performance. Constructive disagreement with organizational policies or decisions is encouraged. Focus is on accomplishing the work.
Career models and systems:		
Values regarding desired direction of career development	Career development process emphasizes vertical advancement and promotion.	Career development emphasizes work experiences tailored to individual goals and needs.
Succession planning emphasis on organizational needs or individual aspirations	Assessment and development focus on predetermined skills and competencies required for particular target positions.	Assessment and development are tailored to desired skills and competencies derived from individuals' own goals.
Succession planning opportunities for individual participation	Succession planning is a centralized activity that involves individuals only after a target position is identified.	People can learn of potential position vacancies, participate in evaluating them, and identify their preferences.
Career track alternatives and flexibility	Career progress is defined as a progression to broader management responsibilities and higher hierarchical levels.	Career progress is defined according to individual growth needs and can take many forms.
	Parallel career tracks are not available.	Parallel career tracks, such as technical tracks, are available.
Values and assumptions regarding ambition and success	Norms and beliefs about success and competence assume that the "best" people are those who want to, and do, make it to the top.	Norms and beliefs about success and competence do not equate success and competence with making it to the top.

Source: Balancing Act, by Joan Kofodimos. Copyright © 1993 by Jossey-Bass Publishers. Permission to reproduce and distribute material, with © notice visible, is hereby granted. If material is to be used in a compilation that is for profit, please contact the publisher for permission.

what it takes to succeed and move up, we may allow the organization to define the terms of our personal development. Thus, our managerial "development" and "success" become defined in relation to the organization's objectives.

Executives' and managers' development in their organizations is channeled through two vehicles. In the short term, development is geared toward the criterion of *current job performance*. That is, we develop ourselves to fit the competencies and skill profiles associated with desired performance in our current jobs. In the long term, development is shaped according to the criterion of *career development:* we define our development by ticking off the development benchmarks involved in vertical ascent up the career ladder. These processes in combination lead us to subordinate our own internally derived visions for ourselves to organizationally determined requirements. The shape of our ideal image is supplemented and reinforced by organizationally valued qualities, and our desire to become our idealized image is strengthened by the promise of upward movement and what it represents.

Externalized Sources of Job Performance Criteria

Although many observers claim that senior executives and managers do have latitude in shaping their jobs to fit their strengths, weaknesses, and inclinations, they do not have much latitude in most organizations to determine the measures on which they are evaluated.[14] It is made quite clear, through performance standards, measurements, and reward systems, what behaviors and results are expected of them. The expected behaviors are generally mastery oriented (such as emphasis on logic, high standards for others, demeanor of confidence), as we saw in the last chapter. And, as we also have seen, executives and managers want to do well in order to receive the psychological rewards that matter to them—whether they involve power, achievement, or a sense of belonging. As a result, they are faced with a dilemma. Success may require emphasizing mastery-oriented values, attitudes, and behaviors, even though doing so might involve compromising some personal beliefs and values to achieve organizational goals.[15] In particular, we saw that Ed Santiago experienced discomfort conducting layoffs in what he saw as an insensitive manner. The mastery-oriented role involved seeing employees in terms of their resource value or financial cost to the organization, rather than worrying about where those employees' next house payment would come from. In organizational terms, the fact that this act was painful and anxiety-provoking to Ed got in the way of his ability to carry out a necessary task. Similarly, Michael Bono commented that when he had to support policies with which he did not agree, he felt as if he were donning a "porcupine's coat," as he put it—a hard prickly shell under which he hid when undertaking distasteful duties.

But, uncomfortable as he was, Bono did carry out those policies. Both he and Santiago suppressed their compassion and empathy, obeying and conforming to their superiors' wishes—and being rewarded for being good team players. Thus, managers and executives face a danger. If in order to succeed in organizations they must focus on power, control, and rationality, then they may lose access to the humanistic urges that come from the intimacy-oriented side of the self.[16]

Thus, the organizational assumption that effective performance primarily involves mastery-oriented qualities encourages our construction and pursuit of an idealized image. This happens, first, because the emphasis on a circumscribed set of skills and attitudes causes us to suppress aspects of our selves that conflict with the desired profile. Second, the very aspects of ourselves that we close off are those that would have equipped us to listen to our own personal values and needs, such as the capacity for deep interaction with others, the expression and revelation of vulnerabilities, or the preference for contemplation. Furthermore, if our effectiveness requires demonstrating a predefined set of mastery-oriented qualities, the possession of which is determined by others' assessment that we have them, then who has the power to decide what qualities it takes for us to be good and worthy? Who has the power to decide whether we have those qualities? Those others have the power to determine these things. Hence, we are in danger of losing control of the conditions of our own self-esteem.

Thus, as managers and executives we face a paradox. We are told our job is to be decisive, to take charge, and be in control. But, at the same time, we experience the real locus of control in organizations—control over events and control over our own worthiness—as outside and above us. We are measured by those above us, on the basis of how well we carry out their strategies. We plan our actions with an eye to managing the perceptions of those above us, so that they will bestow success upon us. This perception of the control as existing in those senior to us keeps the fire of ambition burning, because if we can just get high enough we will eventually feel in control and free from scrutiny and judgment. We do not feel free to acknowledge this dilemma, though, because in order to be perceived as "valuable," we must maintain the illusion that we are, and feel, in control.

Other forces operate in organizations to put the ownership of criteria for effective performance outside us. For example, executives and managers frequently describe to me the mixed messages they receive regarding their roles, performance expectations, and criteria for success. They are told that teamwork is important, for example, but little attempt is made to measure whether they engage in teamwork. Instead, their actual performance is evaluated according to how well they "make their numbers," as some companies refer to the quantitative measurements and standards that prevail.

Similarly, executives and managers tell me they do not experience straight communication about how they are assessed by senior executives who are making decisions about their future. Or, expectations regarding executives and managers' roles or functions are dramatically changed without their input. For example, in one professional firm, a restructuring radically shifted the role of senior consultants. They had joined the firm for the opportunity to apply their technical and analytical skills and preferences, and had risen on the basis of these abilities. In the new organizational design, these people became responsible for selling new business, a set of skills with which most felt unfamiliar and unskilled. The conditions for their success had dramatically changed, and losing the mastery they had previously experienced through work had a tremendously negative impact on them.

Thus, the design and functioning of organizations often make it difficult for us to achieve real mastery based on assessing our talents, skills, and goals in carrying out our role, and deciding what internally derived criteria we hold important and choose to employ in assessing our own level of effectiveness.

Career Models That Verticalize Growth

The way in which organizations construe individual careers over time—the appropriate progression of jobs and kinds of personal development involved in preparing for and successfully carrying out those jobs—also encourages self-idealization. It does so by imposing a restrictive, upward-oriented model of human growth and development. This process occurs as a result of several aspects of career development systems.

First, most career development systems in organizations are constructed vertically. The assumption is that an individual's growth and progress can be reflected in upward movement through hierarchical levels. [17] This, of course, plays right into our underlying feelings, discussed earlier, that higher in the organization means better and closer to our ideals for ourselves.

Second, the process of career development typically involves determining the direction of an individual's development according to the organization's needs and future position requirements. Career planning and development are seen as integrally linked to succession planning, in which the organization member is assessed and developed according to a set of skills and competencies required for effectiveness in future target positions. Some effort is made in human resources practice to "integrate individual and organizational needs," as it is usually called, but in practice individual needs may only be integrated to the degree that they must be in order for the individual's motivation to be maintained. The organization's needs are key and determine the succession planning system's overall structure; individual needs are taken into account when tweaking that overall structure.

Third, this career movement upward and through organizationally determined developmental paths occurs through the designation of upward "tracks," which, except for the occasional "broadening" experience, pattern the individual's development. This tracking essentially renders the individual a passive object, evidenced by the common metaphor of the manager as a "resource" or "asset."

These systems and practices regarding performance standards and career development are so deeply embedded in organizational culture that we take them for granted. We construe them as essential to organizational functioning, and they are essential within the parameters of current organizations. To the extent that we, as organizational members, accept self-idealizing organizational practices, they are destructive to our healthy development. Rounded and healthy individual growth and development will involve challenging these structures and expectations.

four

Choosing Personal Balance: How and Where to Start Changing

If you have been reflecting on your own life and completing the personal assessment exercises in Chapters One through Three, you probably have a growing sense of the state of balance or imbalance in your life. At this point you may feel content, or you may feel a need to change the ways you structure priorities and approach decisions. That is the first step toward constructive change: a dissatisfaction with your current life state, a sense of discrepancy between the kind of life you have now and the kind you want to have.

But there is a long way to go, and the path to change is difficult. When we try to change our behavior, our thinking, our values, we are likely to experience tremendous pressures to remain the same. The phenomenon of inertia makes it simply easier to go on as we have been. Changing will inevitably involve uncertainty, the fear of losing the strengths and skills we have worked so hard to develop. Some peoples' pasts may be strewn with the litter of ambitious developmental intentions from previous workshops, books, and other experiences, which initially led to insight, excitement, and even concrete action plans, but which later faded as the reality of changing turned out to be too much trouble in the face of ongoing everyday demands.

Change takes time. If we choose the path to change, we cannot expect to become balanced tomorrow or next week. We are likely to be seeking change within a number of systems—both organizational and family—that remain (at least for a while) as they were, that experience our changing as disruptive to their stability, and that thus exert pressure on us to stay as we were. And the kind of change involved in balancing our lives requires not only addressing our behavior but also the values and needs underlying our behavior. Such deep inquiry requires special courage. All of this suggests that, if we want to change our life toward balance, we must be very clear in our desire to change and very committed in our intention to follow through with it. To sustain the change process through all the conflicting pressures and pains we will face, we must hold foremost in our mind what we stand to gain, and we must want that more than we want the kind of life we will be giving up. We must also not forget what we stand to lose if we do not change.

Furthermore, the traditional mountain climbing metaphor we have all learned for mastery-oriented goal setting won't work here: the "mountain" image requires us to "set lofty goals and tromp arduously uphill" toward them, relying on "intestinal fortitude" to keep going.[1] Peter Vaill, a noted management writer, has developed an image that will serve us better: the notion of "permanent whitewater," which requires a guiding vision, an "internal locus of stability," to sustain us as we continuously negotiate and manage the moment-to-moment challenges of living in a balanced way.[2]

As we have seen, balance is an issue with both personal and organizational implications. Thus, change must transpire at both levels. This chapter will focus on how we as individuals can address the imbalance issues in our own lives in ways that fit our unique needs and life structures. Ultimately, however, none of us can do this alone. We must also become change agents, influencing the systems in which we live, creating collective changes toward balance in our organizational environments. This turning of our energy outward toward organizational change will be the focus of Chapter Six.

Integrating balance in our own lives involves three levels of change:

1. Balancing our time, energy, and commitment
2. Integrating mastery and intimacy in our approach to living
3. Developing awareness of our real self values and aspirations

The process of change involving these three levels must evolve through natural stages. First, we must evaluate our current life structure and approach to living and their origins clearly and honestly (assessment). Second, we must clarify what we want our life to look like (vision). And third, we must develop concrete strategies for moving from our current life situation toward our vision and for living a life consistent with that vision (change strategies).

If we integrate the three levels of personal change and the three stages of the change process, we end up with a flow depicted in Figure 4.1. This flow represents a developmental process in which each phase creates a readiness for the next phase. Moving through this developmental process will be like peeling an onion, layer by layer, starting with the outermost layer. In the following discussion, we will describe each phase in the sequence. For each phase, there is a corresponding exercise that will help you reflect on how the issues at that level apply to you. It is intended that you work through those exercises as you read the chapter, so that personal insights can build successively.

Assessment

Chapters One, Two, and Three provided beginning opportunities to assess yourself and gain insight by reading about others and by completing the exercises included in each chapter. If you worked through the exercises as you went along, you have a head start on your self-assessment. If you haven't worked through the exercises presented thus far, you may want to do so now before proceeding.

Phase 1: Current Structure of Time, Energy, and Commitment

The key issues or questions addressed here include the following: What is the state of the key spheres in your life right now? How is your current situation a positive one? What are the costs of your current situation?

Chapter One provided a framework for self-assessment on the time-and-energy imbalance issue. The Life Spheres Assessment (Exercise 1.1) provided questions to help you diagnose the state of your

Figure 4.1. Flow of Personal Development Toward Balance.

Level of Balance/Imbalance

The Developmental Challenge	Balancing Time, Energy, and Commitment	Integrating Mastery and Intimacy	Developing Self-Awareness and Self-Realization
	Phase 1	Phase 2	Phase 3
Factors to Assess	Structure of commitments	Approach to living	Aspirations for self
Key Question	How are my time, energy, and commitment allocated among the key spheres in my life?	What are my behavior and approach to living in both work and personal life?	What is the idealized image I am trying to live up to?
Tools	Life Spheres Assessment	Checklist of Mastery- and Intimacy-Oriented Characteristics	Ideal Image Portrait
	Phase 6	Phase 5	Phase 4
Components of the Vision	Vision of central life priorities	Vision of approach to living	Vision of personal aspirations

Stages of the

Change Process

	Phase 7	Phase 8	Phase 9
Key Question	What priority commitments following from my values and aspirations will I structure my life around?	To live consistently with my personal values and visions, what approach to living do I envision?	What are the deep values, goals, and dreams that give me a sense of life purpose and vision?
Tools	Priority List	Approach to Living Vision	Personal Aspirations Worksheet
Change Strategies	Structuring life in accordance with priorities	Implementing mastery- and intimacy-oriented approaches	Living consistently with life values and goals
Key Question	How can I act consistently with my priority commitments?	How can I implement an appropriate balance of mastery- and intimacy-oriented approaches in my key life spheres that enhances the quality of each sphere?	How can I live on an ongoing basis consistently with and towards my vision, and true to myself and my deeply held values?
Tools	Priority Action Plan	Approach to Living Action Plan	Principles for Living Toward Life Vision

life in terms of six key spheres: work and career, family and intimate relationships, friendship and social life, community involvement, physical self, and mental, emotional, and spiritual self.

If you have not responded to the Life Spheres Assessment, you may want to do so now. If you have already responded to it, now is a good time to look again at how you assessed yourself in light of subsequent insights. You may also consider involving one or a couple of key others in your life, such as a spouse or intimate other, a close friend, or a co-worker who knows you well, and seek their input on the questions posed in this exercise and in others in this book.

As you go through the process of assessing the state of the spheres of your life, you may speculate about the possible reasons for the patterns you find, why certain things are going well and others are not. Part of the answer may lie in your approach to those spheres of life. Let's look at that issue now.

Phase 2: Current Approach to Living

The key issues here include the following: What are your current approaches, behaviors, and attitudes in both your work and your personal life? To what extent, and in what ways, do you strive for mastery? And in what ways do you strive for intimacy?

Chapter Two should have provoked reflection on these issues. Specifically, the Checklist of Mastery- and Intimacy-Oriented Characteristics (Exercise 2.1) provided a format for looking at the extent to which your approach to living reflects a mastery orientation or an intimacy orientation. It allows you to determine which behaviors and attitudes characterize your approach to both work and personal life. Again, it may be helpful to solicit the feedback of others who know you well regarding how they see you along these dimensions.

As you reconsider your responses to the Checklist of Mastery- and Intimacy-Oriented Characteristics and notice the patterns with which you have been approaching all spheres of life, you may begin to see how developing more intimacy-oriented qualities to balance the striving for mastery might bring more success and fulfillment.

You may also begin to anticipate what might be difficult about doing so.

Completing this exercise can also help you to be more aware of the kinds of situations you tend to approach with the mastery orientation and those you tend to approach with the intimacy orientation. Ultimately, you can more consciously choose the approach that is more relevant and helpful to a particular situation.

Phase 3: Current Aspirations for Self and Their Origins

The key issues here include the following: What image of yourself are you striving to live up to? What "shoulds" do you hold for yourself based on lifelong messages of what is good and bad? Where did these idealizations and "shoulds" originate? The objective is to move closer to insight regarding the values, goals, and needs for which you have been taught to strive and to understand how these were instilled in you—superimposed upon your real values, goals, and needs.

This issue of the idealized image was the focus of Chapter Three. The Ideal Image Portrait (Exercise 3.1) provided a format for gaining such insight. This exercise began by asking you to reflect into your past, into your upbringing with your parents and other key adults, and to understand the messages they sent you about what kind of person you were and what kind of person you should be. Talking with your parents or siblings about the questions in this phase may yield useful perspective.

The second part of the exercise focuses on the consequences of these early messages in terms of what you seek for yourself as an adult and for how you now define success. The kind of person you strive to be and the way you would like others to perceive you reflect your persona, the "good" side of yourself that you like to express and feel you should be. The kind of person you strive not to be and, more indirectly, the qualities that bother you about others, reflect your shadow, the "bad" side of yourself, which you do not want to acknowledge and do not feel free to express.

Vision

Self-insight can be a powerful intervention in itself, as we discover formerly unacknowledged aspects of ourselves and begin to see our lives in new ways. But self-insight is not usually enough to produce lasting change in desired directions. We must also reach a clear vision, a picture of what we want for ourselves. The purpose of the next three phases is to clarify this vision. The flow of these phases moves in the opposite direction than did the flow of assessment. We begin by creating a vision at the deepest level of balance and use this clarity to inform the creation of vision at subsequent levels.

Phase 4: Vision of Personal Aspirations, Values, and Purpose

Now that you have identified the early messages shaping your idealized image for self, you are in a better position to set those aside and reconnect with your real self, asking the following questions: What do you want for yourself? What kind of person are you, really? The objective here is to move away from self-idealization and toward self-realization, establishing a vision for yourself that honors and builds on your deepest beliefs, values, and goals. The Personal Aspirations Worksheet (Exercise 4.1) is intended to take you through a thinking process that will reveal these deeply held hopes and dreams for yourself and your life. It is designed to help you begin to build your own personal definition of success, balance, and fulfillment.

Phase 5: Vision of Approach to Living

In order to live consistently with the values and aspirations you have identified, you must revisit the way you have been approaching work and relationships. What kinds of behaviors and attitudes, what mix of intimacy-oriented and mastery-oriented approaches to work and personal life, will help you live consistently with your values and aspirations? The Approach-to-Living Vision (Exercise 4.2) will help you translate the values and aspirations you just identified into behaviors and attitudes that you can incorporate into the way you approach life and work. As you do this exercise, try to focus especially on intimacy-oriented approaches, which might be the most difficult to identify.

Exercise 4.1. Personal Aspirations Worksheet.

Reflect on and jot down your responses to the following items.

Childhood dreams

As a child, I fantasized that I would become _____ when I grew up.

The reason this appealed to me was:

How I best enjoyed spending my free time:

Alone, or with others:

The people I most enjoyed being with, and why:

My favorite pursuits, activities, and toys, and why:

Favorite places, and why:

My favorite subjects:

My happiest memories:

Current dreams and fantasies

Something I have always fantasized about doing, but never have done because it was impractical or the right time never came:

If I only worked half-time, I would spend the other half of my time:

If I had a year to live, I would spend it:

Exercise 4.1. Personal Aspirations Worksheet, Cont'd.

Life vision statement

Based on your responses to the above items, the following items give you an opportunity to summarize your vision and mission for your life. Select a year in the future, far enough away that you can make major changes in your life and close enough that you will have many years ahead of you from that time onward—somewhere between five and twenty years from now. Note the year: _____ . From that vantage point, make statements about:

The kind of person I am:

The major elements in my life:

The difference I am making (to others, to the broader community):

How the people closest to me see me:

The most rewarding experiences I am having:

My talents and unique qualities that I am using and building in pursuing my vision:

The meaning of success to me:

Exercise 4.2. Approach-to-Living Vision.

In the left hand column, list the key elements of the life aspirations you identified in the Personal Aspirations Worksheet. In the right-hand column, note some new kinds of attitudes and behaviors, *particularly intimacy-oriented ones*, that will allow you to live consistently with and toward those aspirations. Here is a sample:

Life aspirations (from 4.1)	*Corresponding approach to living*
(projecting myself into the future and looking back over my life, the difference I made in the world and the most special accomplishments, relationships, and events)	*(the kinds of attitudes and behaviors that will be required in order to carry out these life aspirations)*
• Built a world-class research group which developed several disease-curing drugs	• More collaborative with other teams • Listen to others' input • Get help or support when needed
• Developed and mentored a team of crack scientists	• Seek to understand subordinates and their aspirations, give feedback
• Participated in a lifelong mutually growth-enhancing marital relationship	• Get self-esteem from connectedness, value intimate interaction
• Raised happy and healthy children; maintained a satisfying relationship	• More playful and spontaneous • More tolerant of others' needs
• Nurtured my creative and artistic streak	• Able to pursue interests without concern for excelling
• Lived a long, healthy, vital life	• Take time for physical self

Create your own lists here.

Life aspirations	*Corresponding approach to living*

Phase 6: Vision of Central Life Priorities

The key issue here is choice. What few priorities will you choose and commit to that reflect your values and aspirations? Which life areas, relationships, and activities are most important to you and fit best with your values and purpose?

Your key life priorities should flow easily from the values and aspirations you have established and the attitudes and behaviors you have chosen to develop. The Priority List (Exercise 4.3) gives you a structure for defining these key priorities. This exercise is intended to flow from the visions you established for yourself in Phase 4 (your personal values and aspirations) and Phase 5 (your desired approach to living).

It also may be useful to reflect back on Phase 1 and the Life Spheres Assessment to make sure you have not left out any crucial areas or activities. For example, you might discover that you have not established any priorities related to your physical self. If this is an area that you have neglected in the past, you might ask yourself whether physical fitness if something you wish to include as part of your vision for yourself.

As you build your priority list, you might think about balancing a diversity that reflects the varying sides of yourself with a strong and clear focus that reflects your personal values. You might also think about balancing your commitment to others and shared activities with your commitment to taking care of yourself.

Change Strategies

Now that you have a clear picture of your current state of balance and a clear vision of what you want for yourself, the next step is to identify concrete ways of moving toward that vision and living consistently with it.

Phase 7: Plans for Structuring Life in Accordance with Key Priorities

What will you do to behave consistently with your commitment to the key life priorities you have just established? Developing action

Exercise 4.3. Priority List.

Take the list you made in the Approach-to-Living Vision (Exercise 4.2) and, for each item, identify the key life priority that follows from the aspiration and corresponding approach to living. List these priorities in the third column. Here is a sample:

Life aspirations (from 4.1)	Corresponding approach to living (from 4.2)	Key life priorities
(projecting myself into the future and looking back over my life, the difference I made in the world and the most special accomplishments, relationships, and events)	*(the kinds of attitudes and behaviors that will be required in order to carry out these life aspirations)*	*(the priorities that follow from my aspirations and desired approach to living that I choose to commit to and structure my life around)*
• Built a world-class research group that developed several disease-curing drugs	• More collaborative with other teams • Listen to others' input • Get support when needed	• Focus career development within technology function, look for broader and more varied responsibilities there
• Developed and mentored a team of crack scientists	• Seek to understand subordinates and their aspirations, give feedback	• Continue leadership role in technology mentoring program
• Participated in a lifelong mutually growth-enhancing marital relationship	• Get self-esteem from connectedness, value intimate interaction	• Take time to build relationship with partner; play and talk together
• Raised happy and healthy children; maintain a satisfying relationship	• Playful and spontaneous • Tolerant of others' needs	• Spend evenings and weekends with children talking and sharing activities
• Nurtured my creative and artistic streak	• Able to pursue interests without concern for excelling	• Pursue my lifelong interest in painting
• Lived a long, healthy, vital life	• Take time for physical self	• Bicycle three times a week

Exercise 4.3. Priority List, Cont'd.

Now make your own lists.

Life aspirations (from 4.1)	Corresponding approach to living (from 4.2)	Key life priorities

plans will help you to move toward your vision of life balance. Use the Priority Action Plan (Exercise 4.4) to apply the following guidelines to the key life priorities you identified in Phase 6.

Make the priority *clear and specific*. For example, simply stating "my family" as a priority leaves plenty of room for ambiguity. Instead, clarify what it is about your family that is important to you. "To share in my children's activities and accomplishments," "to spend enjoyable leisure time with my partner," and "to develop a network of friends linked by our mutual hobby" are examples of clear and specific priorities.

Make your commitment to that priority *public*. This can increase the likelihood that you will stick with the commitment. For example, you might choose to call a meeting, write a letter, or join a club or association.

Demonstrate your commitment by how you *schedule your time*. Where you devote your time indicates your level of commitment, your goals, and your desire to connect with significant others in your life. Scheduling time includes planning how you will make trade-offs between competing activities. If you have identified "sharing in my children's activities and accomplishments" as a priority, then you might decide that when you must choose between your child's school play or soccer game and a business dinner, you will skip the business dinner. Scheduling also includes establishing boundaries. For example, if you have established "developing a network of friends who share my hobby" as a priority, then you may decide not to accept work-related phone calls during the evenings when those friends are gathered at your house.

- *Eliminate or limit nonpriorities.* Once you have chosen your priorities, you can identify the superficial life areas, relationships, and activities on which you are spending your precious time and energy, the activities that do not move you toward your vision. Find ways to eliminate or reduce them so you can do justice to the few very important ones. For example, you may find that your time is sapped by attending "social" business events. You may decide to stop attending these altogether or to drastically reduce your attendance to a select few. That means eliminating activities that do not contribute to who you are and

Exercise 4.4. Priority Action Plan.

Develop a separate action plan for each of the key priorities you identified in the Priority List. Be sure that each plan addresses each of the following points:

- What is the priority?

- How will you make the commitment public?

- How will you schedule your time?

- What nonpriorities can you eliminate or reduce?

- What support will you seek?

- What development will you engage in?

- What special events will you create?

- What obstacles may you encounter?

- What benefits will you receive?

what you value, not necessarily those that are "unproductive" according to prevailing social assumptions. Taking nature walks might be "unproductive" in terms of tangible output but key to your personal well-being. In contrast, washing the car or mowing the lawn may be activities you do not value and can hire someone else to do, thereby freeing time for the nature walk.

- *Get support from significant others.* There are likely to be many people in your life—friends, family members, and close colleagues—who can provide you with help and feedback. You can take advantage of that help by doing things such as contracting with them for the changes you plan. You may want to collaborate with them on planning these change strategies. In addition, they can give you valuable feedback on what you are currently doing that helps or inhibits your effectiveness in key life areas. Alternatively, you might look for outside support resources such as Workaholics Anonymous or other twelve-step groups.
- *Seek development.* If you are trying to build a formerly neglected life area, you may choose to engage in developmental activities that will help you learn and increase your fulfillment in those relationships and tasks. For example, you might look for a workshop, a support group, or a counselor to help you deal with the new skills and experiences involved.
- *Create special events to support your commitments.* For example, you can use your vacations to pursue other interests such as nature and adventure. You can explore the possibility of taking a sabbatical to pursue interests such as social service or further education. You can set aside weekly time for "minivacations" to do nonroutine things you find enjoyable, such as going on picnics or visiting art galleries. Or, you can set aside unstructured "free time" to spend with significant others or by yourself.
- *Anticipate obstacles and plan how you will address them.* For example, you might expect organizational pressures against your changing. Test this expectation. If you have decided you will avoid going into the office on Saturdays but think this will be frowned upon, stay away from the office for one Saturday and see what happens. Or tell your co-workers of your decision and

listen to their response. Similarly, expect resistance from within yourself to making choices. Remind yourself that the priority areas of your life are interconnected and synergistic, not conflicting. Finally, expect some awkwardness and tension as you begin to revitalize neglected areas of your life. For example, friends and family members may take the opportunity to express anger regarding how you have related to them in the past. Respond by demonstrating your new commitment and understanding their anger. Remember, they may have heard these promises before! Their behavior will change as they see you change your approach and behavior.

•   *Identify the benefits of changing, and keep these uppermost in your mind.* Remember what you stand to gain by balancing; keep an overarching vision of your life as a whole in mind. Think about how spending time and energy in one arena—say, with your family or in meditation—can enrich other arenas, such as your contribution to work or your health.

Phase 8: Plan to Implement Both Mastery- and Intimacy-Oriented Approaches

The key issues here include the following: How can you practice, learn, and become comfortable with the range of mastery- and intimacy-oriented behaviors and attitudes that you have envisioned for yourself? How can you develop new approaches that support your fidelity to the key life priorities you have identified?

Your change strategies regarding this issue will come from your envisioned approach to living and your set of life priorities. Refer to Exercise 4.2, which describes your desired approach to living, and Exercise 4.3, which describes your key life priorities. The challenge in this phase is to anticipate specific opportunities in which you can apply the desired approaches to living in the priority areas of your life. Exercise 4.5 depicts a matrix that allows you to identify such opportunities. For each of the life priorities you have identified, think about how each of the intimacy-oriented approaches you have identified might be applied to that life priority.

You may find it useful in this process to enlist key others in work and personal life as coaches and feedback-givers. As you try

Exercise 4.5. Approach-to-Living Action Plan.

Intimacy-oriented approaches that fit with my life aspirations
(from Exercise 4.2)

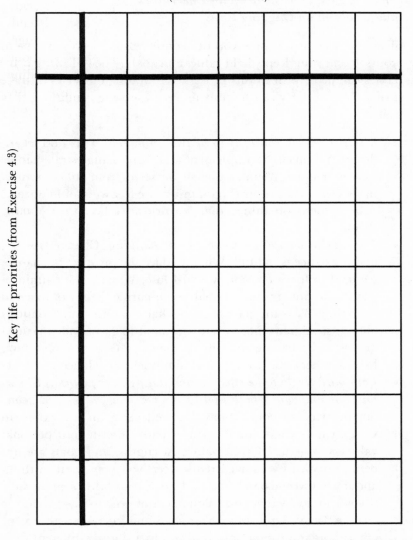

Key life priorities (from Exercise 4.3)

these new behaviors, pay attention to the responses of others as well as to your own reactions and feelings.

Phase 9. Live Consistently with Life Values and Goals on an Ongoing Basis

The key issue here is how you can continually seek to stay true to yourself and your deeply held values and goals. The following principles can be helpful in this process. Reminding ourselves of these principles regularly can help us move toward the conditions they reflect.

- *My first responsibility is to be true to myself.* This notion underlies our ability to implement all of the change strategies we have developed. We must liberate ourselves from our own internally generated pressure to do things we feel we should do, and instead focus on things that are priorities because we value them.
- *It's okay to be apprehensive about changing.* Change is scary, and resistance is natural. When we face the prospect of change, we tend to focus on what we will lose. When we are afraid of change, we justify and rationalize our current behavior to avoid changing. We want to go back to what is familiar and comfortable. Instead, remember what you stand to gain, and what you are losing by leaving your life the way it is. Get the support and help of others. Reaffirm your commitment to balance.
- *I am most likely to be effective and happy in my work if I focus on a job and career path that fit my personal values and goals.* Staying true to yourself involves reflecting on the extent to which your current job and career path fit with your personal values and goals. If your values, strengths, and goals are not being satisfied by your current career, you may want to think about what would be a better fit. Pursue possibilities on the side, if you can, to try them out. You may not need to make a drastic change. Rethinking your career goals and interests within your current organization might lead you to a slightly different path that would be a better fit.
- *I honor and value myself for who I am, strengths and weaknesses alike.* Our life balance is ultimately rooted in an aware-

ness and appreciation of our real self. Thus, finding balance will involve confronting the idealized images that lead to the pursuit of illusions of success. If you love, honor, and tolerate yourself, you will be more tolerant of others, you will handle stress and mistakes better, and you will resolve problems more easily. Honoring yourself means realizing you do not have to struggle for others' approval. Secure in this, you can develop your own priorities and values and take responsibility for your own choices. When you begin to let go of the shoulds, you may feel rudderless and insecure, as if your identity is dissolving. But only then will you be able to separate the dreams and beliefs that are really yours from those that were inculcated by others and your environment in the past.

- *I seek progress, not perfection, on the journey to a balanced life.* The process of changing must be consistent with the goals. How you conduct yourself on the journey is the point, rather than whether you reach a definite goal. Think of success and fulfillment as lying within this open-ended process, rather than in a discrete experience or tangible goal. This is why I have not emphasized concrete milestones or time frames. Our goals and plans here are for every day, starting today and until we decide to revisit our priorities.

- *I welcome mistakes and failures as opportunities for learning.* Failures give us data. We can learn from what went wrong, move on, and prevent it from happening again. If, for example, you have promised that you will put important family events first and then you miss your daughter's birthday party in order to finish a proposal, don't beat yourself up—but don't ignore it, either. Look at the chain of events that led you to violate your commitment. How can you anticipate such conflicts in the future, and how can you plan your time in advance so that you get the work done in time to get to the family event?

- *I live my life every day to be consistent with my values and visions.* Whatever changes you decide on, do not put them off. This is important whether it involves travel, taking it easy, or learning a new skill. None of us knows what will happen to us tomorrow, and you may never get the chance unless you do it now. A friend of mine was driven in her work. Although she always wanted to travel, every year she put it off. She always had just one more work-related crisis, promotion, or responsibility to take care of. Then she discovered she had a degenerative illness and could not know how many years she would continue to be physically mobile. As a result, she realized that she could not forever count on tomorrow. She sold all her possessions and traveled around the world for several years. She returned and decided she would live a balanced life every day. Ten years later, she is happy and healthy and her illness is under control. Is her situation any different from those any of us face? Can any of us forever count on tomorrow for living our dreams?

- *I am guided by a vision and a plan, but remain open for spontaneity and unforeseen opportunity.* Trying to control your development of balance too tightly suggests that you are going at it in the same old mastery-oriented way. Think about planning your movement toward balance in a balanced way, by balancing spontaneity and intention, risk and certainty.[3] Furthermore, the danger of a rigid plan is that it pressures you to know what you'll want in the future. Thus, you might resist unforeseen opportunities, or be less prepared for unforeseen forces. To allow for spontaneity and unforeseen opportunity, it is important to preserve free or unstructured time in your life. It is also important to become comfortable with the uncertainty of letting your future emerge.

- *I cannot change toward balance all by myself; I need the support of others.* Think in terms of interdependence. Moving toward balance does not have to be a completely solitary quest. Your important relationships can serve as support. Similarly, you may consider the possibility of getting professional help. Sometimes we are too wrapped up in our illusions, and too fearful about the uncertainty of changing, to make change without help. We may need someone to help us, give us ongoing feedback, prod us, challenge us, support and encourage our changes, help us recognize our own blinders that get in the way of changing. Sometimes the drive for mastery also produces barriers to changing.[4] For this reason, many people find it useful to enlist an outsider—a consultant or therapist—to help them through the change process.

- *Everything I do is a choice.* It is important to take responsibility for yourself and to recognize that you are always making choices, even when you tell yourself you are being pressured or forced by outside influences. Make the choices deliberate. Act on the basis of judgments, rather than habits or assumptions.

- *My quest for a balanced life never ends; the journey itself is the goal.* Be easy on yourself. One of the biggest potential pitfalls in the search for balance is the tendency to apply habitual imbalanced attitudes and behaviors toward trying to reach a goal of balance. The approach you have spent your life learning in hopes of conquering yourself and the world will not work for conquering imbalance. Only taking a balanced approach to the process of changing will work. To this end, do not create another set of perfectionistic expectations around achieving balance by the end of the year. The objective is not to prescribe a new ideal image to live up to. The objective is not for you to "perform" the new balanced role to perfection. The objective is to embark on a process for coming to know, accept, and love yourself, and for taking the initiative to continually build an inner and outer life consistent with you and your needs. Recognize, also, that you will never get "there," that you will never be finished pursuing balance, because your definition of success and fulfillment will always be changing, expanding, shifting.

five

Assessing the Costs
of Imbalance for Organizations

If the exploration of the development of balance as an individual challenge ended at this point, it would be likely to perpetuate a fallacious assumption that appears to be shared among many executives and managers—the assumption that although balance is good for people's personal life and well-being, it is only achieved at the expense of individuals' career success and organizations' productivity and competitiveness.

Let us look first at the issue of career success. We have seen that many people build imbalanced lives in the pursuit of personal career success. Specifically, managers and executives let work consume their time and energy and allow the drive for mastery to dominate their approach to living in order to live up to an idealized, career-successful image that helps them maintain and enhance self-esteem.

The second issue has to do with organizational effectiveness. We have seen that organizational cultures and norms often reinforce the imbalance in executives' and managers' lives. Decision makers in organizations often consider time/energy imbalance to be in their interest, because it means that executives and managers are placing a high priority on working and contributing to the organization. Thus, the assumption is that imbalance functions in the service of organizational effectiveness.

But the benefits of imbalance to organizational effectiveness and career success are illusory; they are more than offset by a number

106

of costs. First and most apparent are the costs of time/energy imbalance in terms of the associated stress, fatigue, and illness, and the potential consequences of the kinds of life crises we examined in Chapter One. But here we focus on another kind of cost: how an individual's need for mastery affects the workplace.

Managers and executives who seek mastery and self-idealization do often get some measure of the career success they desire. They develop many mastery-related capabilities that contribute to effective management and leadership, and they are likely to be rewarded by promotion in the organizational hierarchy. But they also exhibit certain behaviors and attitudes that are destructive to their management and leadership effectiveness. We can see this point with the case of one high-potential manager, Martin Cummings. His situation reveals several general lessons about the profile of the mastery-driven manager and its benefits and costs.

The Case of One Mastery-Driven Manager

Martin Cummings is the head of new product development for a major division of a Fortune 100 company. At age thirty-six, he is seen as destined for a brilliant future, if he can overcome some potentially fatal flaws.

Martin's approach to leadership is in many respects impeccable. The first quality many coworkers note about him as a manager is his drive for excellence, both for himself and his group. He creates a vision and is persuasive and inspiring in communicating that vision to his group. He is thorough and analytical in collecting data and developing strategies to support the vision. He pushes for results. He is seen as entrepreneurial, identifying and pursuing novel directions for the business. He relies on his comprehensive knowledge of the business and its technology, garnered through his training as an engineer. His discipline and emphasis on performance leads him to work extremely hard to accomplish his goals. He is comfortable in his leadership role and even enjoys the influence he wields. He comes across as charming and confident, even charismatic.

Many attribute Martin's prodigious energy level to his ambition, his desire to make it to the top. This very ambition also gets in his way. Martin seems to care most about getting recognition from his superiors and looking good in their eyes, and that focus on appearance gets in the way of achieving the best result. Some co-workers think Martin is overly focused on his own agenda and his own performance at the expense of broader organizational concerns. He fails to build collaborative relationships with his peers in other functions because he sees them as competitors. He also fails, say his direct reports, to give them credit for their good ideas and work when superiors are pleased with the group's output, and to support them in the face of superiors' criticism.

Martin's need to be right, which leads him to strive for excellence, also leads him to be unwilling to compromise and to become angry and defensive when others disagree with his ideas or offer their own input. He is frustrated with the slowness of team decision-making processes and with the fact that the outcomes often conflict with the solutions he thinks are best.

The downside of Martin's high expectations for his direct reports is that those who do not measure up are in for rough treatment. He becomes abrasive and argumentative with them, fails to coach or develop them, and does not acknowledge the positive contributions they make. It is as if they can do nothing right.

Martin is, despite his ability to be charming, aloof and detached. He rarely shows emotion, except anger and impatience. His overwhelming need to succeed leads him to be overly intense and uptight, especially when he is worried about his performance. He is rarely relaxed, and is seen as lacking a sense of humor.

The strengths and weaknesses of Martin's style as a leader and manager are tied to his underlying character structure, specifically, his drive for mastery and his idealized image of self.[1] His drive for mastery and idealized image, in turn, are the products of his life history, as we see next.

Martin's drive for excellence was instilled in him by parents who had high aspirations for him. They made it clear that they expected their only son to be a leader. They pushed him to excel academically, and when he did not do well, they engaged him in grueling tutoring sessions. They also encouraged his active involvement in church and Sunday school and in Little League baseball.

Martin was an indifferent athlete, but the team sports experience was part of his parents' model of a future leader's upbringing.

Martin's parents conveyed clearly to him their emphasis on discipline and performance. When he experienced paralyzing stage fright before a school speech competition, Martin recalls that his mother said, "Only weaklings are afraid. Never show your fear, because others will use it against you. No matter how you feel, you must get up and perform, and not show anyone what is really going on inside you." Martin got up, performed while feeling sick inside, and won the speech prize.

Martin also recalled his childhood interest in nature. He had loved to walk in the woods near his house and thought someday he might work in forestry or botany. But his parents scoffed at these notions: walking in the woods was frivolous and unproductive, and there was no future in these pursuits. Martin was special by virtue of his intelligence and the privileges with which he had been raised, and he should become an executive like his father so that others would admire and respect him.

So Martin grew up striving for mastery in the way his parents defined it: perfection according to their values and standards. He must shine and excel, achieve high position, create an image people would admire and respect, perform no matter how he felt, beat out others, and do what it took to earn others' admiration. How he felt and what he wanted were immaterial. And although Martin's parents pushed and prodded him to excel, his efforts never seemed to be quite good enough; his parents always seemed to focus on his inadequacies and on what he needed to do even better in the future.

As a result, as Martin grew up, he would have difficulty knowing who he was and what he wanted for himself. He would spend a good part of his adulthood seeking to meet his parents' expectations, with the unremitting fear that he would never be good enough.

As a manager, the strengths and weaknesses in Martin's style reflect his quest to become the masterful idealized image he has internalized. The specific origin of Martin's self-idealization and his specific managerial style are unique to him. But his case exemplifies some general principles concerning how the drive for mastery and self-idealization influence work effectiveness for better and for worse.

How the Drive for Mastery and Self-Idealization Influence Work Effectiveness

If we look at a large number of executives and managers, we find a wide range of managerial styles, some similar to Martin's and others quite different. But most executives and managers I studied share a number of general style characteristics that both originate in inner drives and are fueled by organizational pressures, and that account for both strengths and weaknesses in carrying out their roles. These characteristics are summarized in Table 5.1.

High Standards for Self and Others

Managers' jobs require them to set and reach high goals and to expect the same from others. Meeting high standards and being surrounded by others who can meet high standards are both parts of the managerial quest to feel masterful and worthy. The danger is that individuals with extremely high standards can be overly demanding, hard to please, and even perfectionistic. They can pressure themselves and others in ways that cause stress and resentment and that are thus counterproductive. They might become impatient and intolerant of people who are less quick than they are. In some cases, they may polarize their co-workers into "competent" and "incompetent" categories, and then discount those whom they have designated as incompetent.

Drive for Results

Managers do not stop at holding high aspirations. They also like to turn those aspirations into reality. They tend to be action-oriented doers. And they want to make a difference, to see concrete results of their labor. One danger of this is that in their drive for immediate action they may optimize short-term outcomes at the expense of long-term considerations.

For example, one manager in charge of a sales and marketing

Table 5.1. Self-Idealization Through Mastery: Effects on Work Behavior.

Characteristics	Benefits	Costs
High Standards for Self and Others	Reach for high goals Draw high performance from others	Overly demanding Perfectionistic Create stress, resentment
Drive for Results	Action oriented Like concrete outcomes Want to make a difference, improve tangibly	Achieve short-term results at expense of long-term ones Impatient with team process Resistance creates delays
Need for Closure	Decisive	Do not reflect on decisions or consider risks/options
Emphasis on Logic	Analytical, technical Decisions based on fairness, logic Cognitive complexity	Do not consider human impact of decisions made Do not express praise or appreciation
Suppression of Stress and Anxiety	Calm, detached Resilient under moderate stress	Bottle up emotions Crack at high stress levels
Aggressiveness	Sublimate; "attack" work Lots of energy	Angry outbursts Rage when thwarted
Need to Be Right	Strive hard to make best decisions	Do not admit mistakes Avoid risks Resist others' input
Tendency to Value and Seek Self-Sufficiency	Able to make tough decisions alone	Do not ask for help when needed
Need for Control	Penetrate, monitor Create control mechanisms to oversee	Hands-on, do not delegate Lose subordinates' ideas and motivation
Comfort with Leadership and Power	Ability to mobilize group to achieve goals	Intimidate others Discomfort sharing power

Table 5.1. Self-Idealization Through Mastery: Effects on Work Behavior, Cont'd.

Instrumental Approach to People	Task-focused interaction Objective view of people's performance	Lack empathy and compassion People feel objectified, manipulated
Self-Confidence	Positive attitude Optimism Create confidence in others	Do not express doubts Arrogance, cockiness Overconfidence
Personable Demeanor	Friendly, amiable Appear at ease socially	Distant, aloof Others feel mistrust
Competitive	Want to be the best	Want to beat others Put need to win first
Concern with Own Performance	Strive to excel and to make group excel	Do not give up good people Do not give others credit Do not cooperate with peers
Adoption of Organizational Values	Discipline in carrying out responsibilities	Personal values undeveloped Ethical judgments based on career benefits
Self-Esteem Tied to Achieving Organizational Objectives	Strive hard to achieve existing objectives	Failure to challenge existing objectives
Identification with Superiors	Do what it takes to meet superiors' objectives	Seek to please superiors at expense of others' needs
Drive to Work Hard	Productive, energetic Dedicated to work accomplishment	Do not relax, have fun with ideas Do not allow creative slack
Serious Adult Demeanor	Take responsibilities seriously	Not playful Do not form comfortable working relationships

function was leading an effort to improve customer relations. He was so impatient to demonstrate tangible improvement in this area that he telephoned key customers to check how well his account executives were doing, thus disempowering his account executives in the eyes of customers and short-circuiting the process—the development of relationships between customers and account executives—that would have provided the biggest long-term improvement in customer satisfaction.

Another danger is that action-oriented executives and managers tend to be impatient with processes they perceive as delaying action, such as team decision making, which they often criticize as cumbersome and unnecessary. Unfortunately, by pushing for action early in the process, they often create delays in implementation because of the resistance they have engendered.

Need for Closure

Managers and executives are decisive. They like to see a decision made and the book closed. Thus, they may not take the time necessary to reflect on the risks of a potential course of action or wait to consider a range of alternative courses of action. For example, a brand manager developing a strategy for a product improvement was impatient to complete the written plan before he heard opinions from the research and development group. As a result, important considerations that affected the time frame for unveiling the product were omitted from the plan.

Emphasis on Logic

Executives and managers rely on finely developed analytical, technical, and logical capabilities. They prefer to make decisions according to what is fair, right, and reasonable. They demonstrate "cognitive complexity," which involves the ability to create order from chaos and to see patterns in data.[2]

However, in their reliance on logic, managers and executives risk being insensitive to others' feelings. They may fail to take into account nonrational factors that turn out to have measurable consequences; for example, they may make logical decisions that hurt or threaten organization members or that organization members may not be willing or capable of implementing. For example, one plant manager selected and implemented an automated production control system, which made eminent sense from a rational point of view. However, he failed to consider the potential for employee resistance, fear, and lack of understanding of the rationale for the proposed system, and he correspondingly failed to consider the importance of getting employees' acceptance and input into the decision. Like many managers, he failed to realize that the impact on people—how people react to a decision—has tangible implications for the ease and quality of the decision's implementation. Similarly, logic-oriented managers may not recognize the importance of giving people such nonlogical motivators as appreciation, praise, and recognition.

Suppression of Stress and Anxiety

Executives and managers often appear to be detached and calm under pressure. This demeanor helps them to be resilient under stress, and it helps others around them feel reassured and confident in their ability to handle difficulties.

The other side of this detachment is that business leaders tend to suppress and deny stress, to "bottle up their emotions," and to ignore symptoms of physical distress. The stress collects inside, gathering pressure. Then, when an event occurs—either a major crisis, such as a spouse leaving or a deal going bad, or a seemingly trivial event, such as a minor traffic accident or a child getting into a scrape—the manager is hit with a sense of loss. "Typically, his response, because he has neglected thinking or feeling on the subject for years, goes way overboard."[3] A response might include altered behavior, such as extreme mood swings, emotional outbursts, drastic performance deterioration, or unexplained absences—all symptoms of depression and anxiety.

Aggressiveness

Managers and executives have high levels of aggressive energy. Aggression is a basic psychic drive, which can be engaged productively and creatively by "attacking" one's work: controlling the work object, dominating it, and transforming it by producing a project or creating a plan.[4] But if the aggressive urge is thwarted, it is often manifested as hostility and rage. Thus we see managers who engage in angry outbursts when something or someone gets in the way of their projects or plans.

Need to Be Right

Managers and executives strive hard to come up with the right answer and make the best decisions. When they are right, they feel competent; they feel they have lived up to their ideals and goals for themselves. Conversely, it is difficult for them to be wrong: to own up to mistakes, to listen to and accept opinions or input that might diverge from their own ideas, to go out on a limb. They are thus often defensive and resistant to critical feedback.

Tendency to Value and Seek Self-Sufficiency

Managers like to rely on themselves; they want to be able to think "I did this" or "I created this." The ability to count on themselves, to be independent, is seen as a sign of strength and self-confidence. Asking for help is a sign of weakness. Thus, they have the fortitude to make tough decisions by themselves. But when help is truly needed, they have a hard time asking for it.

Need for Control

Managers and executives like to be in charge and to have their fingers on the pulse of the organization's activities. They are thus skilled at "penetrating" the organization to tap into what is going on, at monitoring, at creating control mechanisms to oversee and regulate the organization's functioning.[5]

However, in their desire to be in charge, managers and executives are often afraid to let go. They can be stubborn and inflexible. They can be overly hands-on and reluctant to delegate. They can adopt the "do it my way" approach to managing, telling highly skilled direct reports not only what to do but also exactly how to do it. Consequently, they can miss out on potentially better ways of doing things. They also risk diminishing their direct reports' motivation and commitment.

Comfort with Leadership and Power

Managers are comfortable with, and even relish, exerting influence in the service of collective goals.[6] This ability helps them mobilize organizational members to achieve the organization's goals and objectives. But it can also produce managers who throw their weight around and intimidate others or managers who are only comfortable as "top dogs" but are not comfortable sharing power.

Instrumental Approach to People

Managers' interaction with others in the workplace is typically task focused—limited to the topics and formats required by the work to be done. Thus, the manager is able to maintain an objective perspective on individuals and their performance, unclouded by sentiment or other subjective factors. This approach to people as resources, objects, and instruments of task accomplishment, comes at a cost of empathy and compassion. When people feel that they are just "resources," without a deeper level of concern, they may feel manipulated and betrayed, and their most powerful source of commitment—feelings of ownership and being valued—remains untapped.

Self-Confidence

The upbeat demeanor typical of executives and managers, their positive attitudes and optimism, create confidence in others. But executives and managers may become trapped in their own self-induced pressure to always feel and appear confident, so much so that they are unable to express, or even to allow themselves to become aware of, any self-doubts. They will at least jeopardize their own well-being by this mismatch between what is going on inside them and what they are portraying on the outside. Furthermore, extreme confidence can become arrogance and cockiness, which may alienate others. Lacking in humility and the recognition of their own limits, they may assume responsibilities they cannot handle or rush into big mistakes.

Personableness

Managers and executives are often described as friendly and amiable. They have well-developed social skills and appear at ease in gatherings. But their amiability only goes so far. Beyond that point, they are often seen as distant and aloof, which may lead others to feel uncertainty and mistrust regarding what they are actually thinking and feeling.

Competitiveness

Managers and executives strive to win and to thereby prove themselves worthy. In some cases they compete against their own internal standards. In other cases, they compete against others, engaging in one-upsmanship. If they are competing against others in their own organization, they may put the need to win ahead of the organization's needs and objectives. They will not be likely to work collaboratively and cooperatively with peers in the pursuit of shared goals.

Concern with Own Performance

Managers and executives seek recognition. They want to be seen as special in their own eyes and in the eyes of others. Consequently, they strive for their divisions or units to excel. In their desire to look good, though, they may compromise broader organizational considerations. They may be reluctant to give up good people who are ready for promotion or who are needed elsewhere. They may fail to share credit with others who deserve it. They may have difficulty cooperating with other departments. They may become empire builders instead of team players.

Adoption of Organizational Values

We have seen that executives and managers put their career requirements above their other personal needs—for intimate relationships, leisure, and so on—because career success is what gives them mastery. In their focus on mastery via career success they adopt the operative values of the organizations in which they wish to succeed. They are disciplined in carrying out their responsibilities, subordinating personal needs that might conflict with the needs of their careers in the organization. Such martyrdom cannot succeed in the long term because personal needs eventually "leak out" if they are suppressed long enough, often in a destructive manner. Thus, for example, by neglecting needs for intimacy, managers may end up entangled in office affairs that lead to conflicts of interest. Furthermore, by ignoring the development of their personal values, they become susceptible to flaws in ethical judgment. Their only ethical criterion becomes "What is best for company success and thus for my success?"

Self-Esteem Tied to Achievement of Organizational Objectives

Managers and executives come to identify with the organization and thus strive hard to achieve its objectives, according to the existing system of organizational measurements. Thus they may not be able to step outside this system and challenge measurements, norms, and policies that are inconsistent with organizational visions and values or with other criteria, such as social or environmental responsibility.

Identification with Superiors

Managers and executives want to advance, to move into their superiors' shoes. They also want to be esteemed by their superiors. Superiors' approval is important because their opinion is relevant to promotion decisions, because they have attained the qualities necessary to achieve their high position, and because they symbolize the authority figures from childhood whose approval is needed in order to feel worthy.

Therefore, executives and managers seek to please their superiors by doing what it takes to meet their superiors' objectives. They may do so at the expense of the needs or requirements of peers, direct reports, and external stakeholders.

Drive to Work Hard

Executives and managers like to be productive, and they feel wasteful when they are "idle." Thus, they are energetic and dedicated in the pursuit of work accomplishment. They are also uncomfortable relaxing in the context of work, batting ideas about with colleagues with no particular goal, or setting unresolved ideas aside to simmer on the back burner—all activities that are essential to creativity.

Serious, Adult Demeanor

Managers and executives take themselves and their responsibilities seriously. Play is frivolous and therefore not allowed. However, applying a playful approach to work problems is often exactly what is needed to free up the thinking process and brainstorm novel solutions. Similarly, joking and being lighthearted with coworkers can lubricate working relationships and increase comfort in working together.

In sum, managers' and executives' behavior at work is shaped by the same internal wishes and needs that lead to imbalance in work and personal life: their drive to feel and appear masterful in the service of living up to an idealized image. These leaders' ambitions and goals for their organizations reflect their ambitions and goals for themselves, and their approach to mobilizing their organizations to achieve those ambitions and goals reflects their approach to reshaping themselves to fit the qualities of their idealized images of self. They seek external validation of their worth through recognition by others, advancement up the organizational hierarchy, and others' admiration and respect. We might say that they put the organization's needs above their own—but what they are really putting first are their own careers and their unconscious need to prove their worth to themselves and others. Thus, in the guise of sacrificing their needs to the company's they surreptitiously meet their unacknowledged needs to feel masterful and worthy.

     That managers' and executives' seeming dedication to their organizations often disguises a deeper dedication to their own needs only becomes obvious when there is a conflict between what is best for the organization and what is best for the individual's experience of mastery. For example, one manager's image of himself as invincible led him to pursue an acquisition that carried hidden downsides he had not bothered to investigate and that lost his company millions of dollars. Another engaged in illegal activities to carry out a superior's mandate, which, when discovered, led to the company's having to pay a hefty fine to the government.

How Change Poses Threats to the Mastery-Oriented Manager

Certain situations are especially likely to provoke and exaggerate the conflict between the individual's drive for mastery and the effectiveness and health of the organization. These situations are all related to change in some fashion; either change of one's own position or change in the business environment. The mastery-oriented manager experiences change as a threat to survival and esteem.

Job Promotion

The higher an individual moves in an organization, the more it is necessary to demonstrate such behaviors and characteristics as supporting and developing direct reports; receiving gratification from others' successes; delegating and empowering others; feeling comfort with team process; enlisting, listening to, and respecting others' ideas; being sensitive to the impact of one's decisions on others. When the individual seeking mastery receives a promotion and moves into a higher position, his first goal is often to appear competent and on top of things. This might make him prone to over-control at exactly the moment when the opposite is needed. He may be more concerned with how he is doing than with integrating into the new unit and paying attention to its members' needs.

Environmental Turbulence

Constant change is becoming more and more a part of corporate life. And to live with, anticipate, and respond to change, it is important that executives and managers realize that information and ideas can originate anywhere in the organization, that having a formal position does not entail being the first to know about customer needs, new competition and regulations, and other problems and opportunities. Thus, the organizational leaders must learn to value and encourage information sharing and input from all over the organization, without regard to formal position or hierarchical level.

The manager's and executive's loss of real control and mastery in the face of ongoing turbulence is a fact. But it may be difficult to give up the attempt to stay in charge of everything, to remain the hub of information and decision making, and instead to manage in a new role—as a coach, supporter, provider of resources, and communication link.

Restructuring

With the increasing economic pressures in today's business environment, many organizations are implementing leaner structures, which include fewer layers, fewer people, and combined jobs. Managers and executives who were comfortable with previous ways of doing business as usual may now be required to take on new, broadened responsibilities without a corresponding raise in level or pay. If they are reliant on mastery through expertise and control, they may resist the prospect of engaging in activities in which they do not feel proficient, in which they may need to rely on and learn from others' proficiency, and in which they must take on different attitudes and values.

For example, a technical manager who is made part of a multifunctional team that addresses customer service issues must modify the technology-push orientation she has had throughout her career and become concerned with the market's needs. A partner in an accounting firm who has excelled at increasing levels of technical complexity and project management and who now is given responsibility for selling new business must learn skills in marketing and customer service. These kinds of challenges strike at the heart of the manager's fear of appearing weak or incompetent.

High-Involvement Organizations

With the increasing popularity of such organizational innovations as total quality, continuous improvement, and high involvement, there are corresponding changes in the demands of the leader's role.

These innovations tend to give decision making to those who are directly involved in doing the work in question; they solicit input on how to improve tasks across levels and functions, and by doing so, they create a democratic climate in which all members of the organization feel higher levels of ownership and commitment.

When such changes are instituted in an organization, its members are vigilant toward the behavior of their management; they are extremely sensitive to any autocratic or controlling behaviors that might appear to confirm their suspicion that management will not back up their rhetoric with action.

Behavior driven by the quest for mastery is inconsistent with the kinds of behaviors required to support democratic cultures. Mastery-driven managers might, without thinking, denigrate people's ideas, react defensively to suggestions that seem to challenge their own initiatives, maintain sole power of approval for proposals and suggestions, fail to provide reinforcement and reward for individuals' taking on added responsibility, and in general demonstrate an unwillingness to share power. Organizational members lower in the hierarchy will take these behaviors to indicate that democracy and involvement are just a matter of lip service.

Poor Performance

Given the new and increased challenges of carrying out the executive role, managers at all levels are increasingly likely to make mistakes. If a manager who wants to feel and appear masterful is performing poorly, he may find it difficult to admit concern or ask for help. He may be resistant to critical feedback that might point the way to areas for development. Paradoxically, the characteristics of the drive for mastery that underlie such performance problems can also lead to rigid and reluctant behavior in the face of needed change.

Work Setbacks

As new business challenges and tight job markets contribute to increasing performance pressures, it is likely that the average manager and executive will suffer work setbacks. He or she may lose a desired promotion, be demoted, be relegated to a plateau, or even be fired. An individual whose only source of self-esteem is work mastery is not likely to be resilient—to be equipped with coping strategies for handling the threat to mastery attached to such setbacks.

How the Mastery-Oriented Organizational Culture Poses Threats to Our Future

In addition to the challenges it poses to individual effectiveness, the drive for mastery holds broader implications. If we think of organizations as populated primarily by mastery-oriented managers and executives, we can also speculate about the kinds of organizational cultures they will shape and the kinds of broader societal patterns that might emerge as a result.

An organization run by mastery-driven leaders is likely to resemble the traditional bureaucratic organization, with its strict hierarchy of control and decision-making—what Philip Slater refers to as an "authoritarian" organization.[7] It is likely to be characterized by mistrust and by behavior oriented toward satisfying one's superiors and advancing one's career.[8] Relationships among individuals are likely to be competitive and task focused. Anger may be the only acceptable emotion.

Even more broadly, a society dominated by mastery-oriented individuals will be characterized by a valuing of competition, independence, self-reliance, and aggression. These become, as Suzanne Gordon writes, "the organizing principles around which we construct our behavior, ethics, and personal relationships."[9] The focus on these central values leads to what she calls the "social devaluation of caring," the consequences of which we see all around us in the form of homelessness, exploding racial tensions, rising infant mortality, and the beginnings of a health care and insurance crisis that threatens to affect all our lives.

Surely we are in agreement that this is not the kind of world we want to live in or to pass on to our children. But is there another way to lead? And will it still get the job done? Recent research shows that other patterns of leadership exist, patterns not dominated by mastery and self-idealization, and that they can be effective.

The Alternative: A Balanced Leadership Approach

There is evidence that leadership styles incorporating a blend of mastery- and intimacy-oriented behaviors are more effective than leadership styles emphasizing one or the other. For example, a recent article discussed the potential for promoting "nurturing" in organizations. The writers discussed several arguments in favor of this approach: nurturing may encourage increased commitment to organizational objectives and may provide increased opportunities to exercise self-direction; it may enhance productivity because it leads people to feel better about themselves and their organizations; nurturing leadership styles may spur employees to higher productivity; and nurturing may enhance a free flow of ideas and thus improve creativity. [10]

While these assertions about nurturing are largely anecdotal, one empirical study supports them. It assessed the effectiveness of two contrasting modes of leadership, autonomous and interdependent, which are parallel to our mastery- and intimacy-oriented approaches (see Table 5.2). [11] This study found that managers evaluated as high-performing by senior management and seen as effective leaders by their co-workers demonstrated a higher level of both autonomous leadership practices and interdependent leadership practices than did managers in a control group. For example, the single practice most highly correlated with others' perception of effectiveness was "promoting the development of people's talents," an interdependent practice. "Other interdependent practices that emphasized caring, involvement, recognizing contributions, and appealing to people's hearts and minds also correlated highly with effective leadership. This shows that the interdependent practices are central components of the perception of effective leadership." [12]

Ultimately, then, managers and executives will gain not only in their personal lives but also in their work effectiveness if they can learn to balance their mastery-oriented approach to the world with attitudes and behaviors oriented toward intimacy. Organizations, too, will benefit by fostering a culture of balance. One route to such a culture is through the enlightened leader's behavior. Leaders who experience their own transformation and recognize the value of balance in their lives and in their approach to work, are likely to feel

**Table 5.2. A Comparison of Interdependent
and Autonomous Leadership.**

Autonomous leadership	*Interdependent leadership*
1. Leadership is related to position of authority: self is seen as separate from group.	1. Leadership is a function that can shift among group members: self is seen as part of "we."
2. Leader sets and communicates vision and direction: acts as trusted representative; communicates vision well.	2. Leader facilitates the joint creation of vision and direction: acts to integrate and incorporate all views; listens well.
3. Leader acts as problem identifier and solver: uses good analysis to offer solutions.	3. Leader shares relevant knowledge so that group can generate ideas, formulate hypotheses, and test them; leader uses intuition to understand situations.
4. Leader is an objective learner: steps back to understand.	4. Leader is a connected learner: steps into a situation to understand it.
5. Leader shows concern for goal/task accomplishment: committed to duties, organized, efficient; delegates responsibility.	5. Leader shows concern for involvement and development of people: emphasizes interpersonal relationships; shares responsibility.
6. Leader's ethics include fairness, respect for rules and contracts: leader embraces external principles, values, standards; seeks justification by external standards.	6. Leader's ethics include care and responsiveness: leader embraces maintenance and restoration of relationships; seeks justification in the particular context of each situation.
7. Leader's approach to conflict resolution involves compromise of views: encourages reciprocity between separate individuals; uses logic, argument, proof, and contracts.	7. Leader's approach to conflict resolution involves integration of views: encourages balancing needs of self and others; uses dialogue.

Source: Adapted from Bragar, 1990, p. 40. (See note 11.)

that it is incumbent on them to support the development of others whose lives they affect—direct reports, colleagues, family members. Enlightened leaders can also begin to intervene in their organizations to raise general awareness of the importance of balance, and to establish practices and policies for becoming a "balanced" organization.

six

Creating the
Balanced Organization

It should be clear by now that imbalance is not only a problem for individuals but also a problem for organizations. We have seen that imbalance manifested in individual lives affects organizational functioning, even as organizational culture is itself partially responsible for those individual life difficulties. In this chapter, we discuss how those of us who are tired of paying the price for imbalance in our lives, and tired of living in imbalanced organizations, can become change agents and reshape the organizational environment for ourselves and others.

There are two overarching reasons why it is important to change organizations so that they are more consistent with the principles of balance. First, if we value individuals' development toward balanced lives, we must create supportive organizational environments; our individual efforts to find balance are limited and even perhaps ultimately doomed as long as we remain inside imbalanced organizations. Second, if we value organizational effectiveness, a balanced organization is also an adaptive one. The kinds of change that support individual life balance are also crucial to organizations hoping to survive and thrive amid current and future business challenges.

You, the reader of this book, are both the recipient and the carrier of organizational culture. We focus in this chapter on your empowered role as a carrier of culture, as a change agent. Organizational change will depend on you—on your acting differently toward the people whose lives you influence, on persuading others with decision-making responsibility and visibility to recognize balance issues, on initiating and encouraging an organizationwide change process. As you act to change the culture of your organization, you will reap the benefits of living in a changed culture that is more supportive of human values.

The kinds of change discussed here go beyond current organizational approaches to work-personal balance. This is not to denigrate the recent wave of organizational interest in balance-related issues, which has resulted in the increasing popularity of "family-friendly" policies such as child-care benefits, flexible work scheduling, elder care, parental leaves, and wellness programs. It is simply to say that, by themselves, these interventions do not touch the deep-rooted issues we have come to understand as the sources of imbalance, issues such as the fundamental assumptions we hold regarding what it takes to be successful and effective as executives and managers, and as organizations.

Because family-friendly programs by themselves do not address the fundamental sources of imbalance, there are sometimes unintended side effects in organizations that try to implement them. For example, in one company there emerged a two-tiered hierarchy in which the family-oriented "mommy track" employees (who were indeed primarily women) took advantage of family-friendly programs, and the career-oriented, high-potential managers continued to focus on work, as they always had, at most taking advantage of the company's new fitness center. Such side effects occur because family-friendly programs do not typically address organizational norms and values that discourage career-oriented managers' use of those programs. If people who care about career success take advantage of family-friendly programs, and thus visibly establish family and personal life as a priority, they may face unspoken judgments regarding their lack of commitment toward organizational goals, and thus their lack of ultimate promotability potential.

Contributing to the stigma of balance at managerial levels is the reluctance of executives and managers to confront the issue of imbalance in their ranks. This defensiveness regarding their own imbalance makes it difficult for them to understand the importance of balance to others similar to them (for example, other high-level managers). They prefer to define balance in a way that bounds it and confines it to others—as something only "lower-level" people are interested in or as an issue of time management and practical support that can be addressed by policies such as child care for single mothers.[1]

Furthermore, even if family-friendly policies were more fully used by managers, it should be clear that these kinds of interventions, by themselves, would not address the range of issues and forces contributing to imbalance in executives' and managers' lives. For example, a lack of child care is a less fundamental deterrent to a manager seeking balance than is the drive for mastery. Thus, even a manager who has access to a convenient, inexpensive child-care program can still have an unfulfilling personal life if he or she does not know how to relax and be close with others and if organizational life suppresses the development of these capabilities. Thus, addressing imbalance thoughtfully requires not only establishing family-friendly programs but also reducing the emphasis on mastery in the service of self-idealization. That emphasis accounts for the norms that discourage managers from establishing personal life as a priority and from taking advantage of family-friendly programs.

Both surface issues and underlying organizational practices and cultures, then, influence leaders' ability to balance their lives. Organizational change needs to be effected at three levels, which correspond to the organization's role at each of the three levels of imbalance in individual lives:

- Expectations and rewards regarding the organization's role in leaders' networks of time, energy, and commitment
- Nature of the valued leadership profile, in terms of the types of mastery- and/or intimacy-oriented behaviors encouraged in managers and executives
- Approach to integrating organizational aspirations and human development

The *process* of organizational change toward balance is similar to the process of personal change. For example, in both personal and organizational change, we must treat the quest for balance as an ongoing process rather than as a finite project with a start and end point. Similarly, in both personal and organizational change, the energy to carry out *change strategies* is mobilized by a deeply held *vision* and an awareness that there is a gap between the current state, articulated through *assessment,* and that vision.

Personal and organizational change also differ in some respects. To make organizational changes, we must think in terms of leading a process that ultimately involves many people. The shape of a particular organization's movement toward balance evolves through the participation of its members. Thus, as change agents, a large part of our role is to initiate and nurture an organizationwide process that mobilizes other peoples' support for, commitment to, and ownership of change. However, there is also much that we can do individually to promote organizational change, by spreading the word about balance, by engaging in our own personal development and in behaviors that are consistent with balance, and by supporting our co-workers in their pursuit of balanced lives.

The phases of organizational change begin with assessment; establishing a vision is next, and the last is addressing strategies for change. Because the shape of the organizational process ideally will emerge through the involvement of system members, the linear examination of the phases that appears here is largely for explanatory purposes and is not intended to be followed rigidly. What is essential is that all the elements occur: a clear understanding of the current state, the envisioning of a desired future state, and the development of strategies for creating a balanced organization. It is also essential to address the key issues at all three levels of imbalance: time, energy, and commitment; mastery and intimacy; and self-idealization or realization. Figure 6.1 summarizes the flow of the assessment and intervention phases.

Assessment

You may want to engage in the assessment process on your own initially. However, you may find it valuable to bring in other organizational members as early as possible to participate in identifying the current organizational state and how it fosters balance and imbalance.

Phase 1: Current Expectations Regarding
Leaders' Structure of Commitments

The key issues here are the following: To what extent do our organizational culture and norms encourage an imbalanced commitment in which leaders' time and energy are devoted primarily to work? What kinds of assumptions do we hold regarding the capability and dedication of an executive or manager who wants to live a life of balanced commitments? Is this seen as acceptable and healthy behavior or is it seen as demonstrating a lack of potential?

Our organization may value a primary time/energy commitment to work in the form of long office hours, heavy workload, weekend travel, and frequent geographic moves. Or it may value time/energy balance in the form of setting time boundaries on work, establishing personal life as a priority, taking full vacations, and using alternative work schedules and benefits that allow attentiveness to personal life. Or it may fall somewhere between the two extremes.

Exercise 1.2 in Chapter One provides an opportunity to examine the organization's expectations regarding an executive's or manager's structure of commitments. It also encourages us to think about our shared responsibility in shaping organizational culture. We each receive other peoples' expectations; we also convey expectations to other people who depend on us. What messages do we send to them? What level of time/energy commitment to work do we value?

In addition to assessing how the organization encourages a particular allocation of time and commitment, we must look at how the organization supports a particular leadership profile. This occurs in the next phase of organizational assessment.

Phase 2: Current Profile of Mastery- and
Intimacy-Oriented Leadership Practices

The key issues here are the following: What mastery- and intimacy-oriented leadership skills and qualities are valued in our executives and managers? What is our organization's dominant pattern? We can look at the desired profile in terms of the extent to which it

Figure 6.1. Flow of Organizational Intervention Toward Balance.

Level of Balance/Imbalance

The Intervention Challenge	Organization as Part of Network of Balanced Commitments	Leadership Profile Balancing Mastery and Intimacy	Integrating Organizational Aspirations and Human Development
	— Phase 1 —	— Phase 2 —	▶ Phase 3
Factors to Assess	Expectations of leaders' structure of commitments	Profile of mastery- and intimacy- oriented practices	Assumptions about individual development in organizations
Key Question	What level of commitment do we reward and encourage?	What kinds of management and leadership attitudes and behavior do we inculcate?	What values do we hold for integrating managers' development and organizational purposes?
Tools	Organizational Expectations Regarding Time and Energy Commitment	Organizational Climate for Mastery and Intimacy	Cultural Practices Shaping Self-Idealization vs. Self-Realization
	▼ Phase 6	◀ Phase 5	▼ Phase 4
Components of the Vision	Vision of the organization's place in the individual's life structure of balanced commitments	Vision of the desired leadership culture	Vision of the integration between organizational aspirations and human development

Stages of the

	Phase 7	Phase 8	Phase 9
Key Question	How is time/energy balance integral to optimal organizational functioning?	How is a leadership profile that integrates mastery and intimacy integral to optimal organizational functioning?	How is self-realization integral to optimal organizational functioning?
Tools	Dialogue for Building a Vision of Balanced Time, Energy, and Commitment	Dialogue for Envisioning a Mastery- and Intimacy-Balanced Leadership Profile	Dialogue for Envisioning a Culture Integrating Organizational Aspirations and Human Development
Change Strategies	Encouraging managers to balance work and other priority commitments	Encouraging a balance of mastery- and intimacy-oriented leadership qualities	Supporting the pursuit of personal values and mission through work
Key Question	How to create an organization that helps managers identify and act consistently with their priority commitments?	How to create a view of leadership as involving a balance of mastery- and intimacy-oriented approaches that fit with individual preferences?	How to create a culture that helps managers develop toward their life vision in a way that fosters organizational excellence?
Tools	Sample Change Strategies for Creating a Climate for Balanced Time, Energy, and Commitment	Sample Change Strategies for Creating a Climate for a Balanced Leadership Profile	Sample Change Strategies for Creating a Climate for Self-Realization

Change Process

consists of mastery-oriented behaviors (such as focusing on rationality, taking charge, and conveying a demeanor of confidence) and the extent to which it is characterized by intimacy-oriented behaviors (such as focusing on people's feelings and needs, collaborating, and displaying a playful attitude at work).

Exercise 2.2 in Chapter Two provides a format for obtaining a quick sketch of the organization's leadership culture, its balance of intimacy- and mastery-oriented leadership qualities. The assessment can be used in a number of ways. One is to use it to compare how an organization's "typical" and "best" managers approach the leadership role. The "typical" manager's profile indicates the dominant pattern and implies the nature of the dominant organizational culture. The "best" manager's profile indicates behavior and qualities that are especially valued and rewarded. With these two pieces of information, it becomes possible to ask how the "best" managers differ from the "typical" managers, and what the differences imply. For example, looking at these differences may help us understand the discrepancy between the skills and qualities that are desired and those that are actually rewarded and developed in most managers.

Exercise 2.2 can also be given to individual managers as a self-assessment tool so that they can better understand their own leadership styles. Their responses can then be aggregated with those of their co-workers to develop a group profile that can help group members better understand their similarities and differences and their organization's culture and norms regarding leadership. Yet another way to use the assessment is to ask organization members to complete it in answer to the question "What qualities do we look for when we select or promote managers?"

In fact, Exercise 2.2 can be framed around a number of specific questions, depending on the needs and preferences of organization members. The general purpose is to help organization members understand the overall pattern of mastery- and intimacy-oriented leadership qualities in the organization and to reflect on the benefits and costs of this leadership pattern.

The next phase in the assessment process examines the nature of the organization's assumptions and values regarding how

managers' development as people intersects with their development
as managers.

Phase 3: Current Assumptions Regarding the Nature of
Individual Development in the Organizational Context

The key issues here are the following: What are the basic assumptions about and objectives for the development of people in the organization? To what extent do we define developing people in terms
of filling slots, or, conversely, in terms of helping people reach their
own potential? How do we integrate the organization's interests and
individuals' needs? Is individual development subordinated to the
accomplishment of organizational aspirations or are the two held
as co-equal?

Assessment in this area focuses on whether organizational
assumptions regarding development encourage conformity to an
idealized set of qualities or aspirations, or whether they encourage
fidelity to one's true inner self, aspirations, and needs.

Exercise 3.3 in Chapter Three provides a structure for reflecting on the overall culture of your organization and on specific
events you have experienced or witnessed. Your responses will suggest to you the extent to which your organization supports self-
idealization or self-realization.

The exercise assesses organizational practices in terms of two
dimensions. The first is control over performance criteria and the
conditions of one's own success. To what extent do individuals have
input into the criteria of their performance and the design of their
work? How clearly are performance expectations and feedback com-
municated? How valued are individual judgment and integrity as
opposed to conformity to norms?

The second dimension assessed is the nature of career models
and systems. To what extent do career development systems focus
on upward progression as opposed to encouraging personally
valued and driven growth directions? To what extent is succession
planning driven by the availability of positions as opposed to individual aspirations? To what extent are individuals involved in the
succession planning process affecting them? Are parallel career
tracks available? How do we define career success?

Now that assessment has been completed and the organization's current state regarding balance has become clear, the next step is establishing a vision of the desired state.

Vision

There are two key ground rules in establishing a vision for organizational balance. The first is to involve people, lots of people, the whole organization if possible, in creating a vision that is truly shared. The second is to establish a shared and clear conviction of how balance is integral to organizational effectiveness.

The process of creating a vision of what we want our balanced organization to look like is at least as important as the outcome. If the process of crafting this vision gives people a taste of the benefits of working in a balanced culture, it will generate energy for change toward such a culture. To this end, we must build a network of people in the organization who support balance, with whom we can create a shared sense of how we want our organizations and our lives to be. The network must include respected senior leaders as well as opinion leaders at all organizational levels, who support balance and who back up their words with consistent behavior. To the extent that they are pursuing their own personal development toward balance, it is more likely that they will act as positive role models and encourage others to pursue balance.

The vision must include balance as an integral element in the organization's effective performance of its essential tasks. Thus, although we are isolating the idea of balance so that it can take hold in organizations, it must not remain isolated. Instead, it must be integrated into the organizational mission and practices. It must become a part of how things are done in an ongoing way, a concept that is incorporated into the working through of business issues and the making of business decisions. To this end, it is important to envision how balance contributes to organizational effectiveness and achieving strategic business objectives. If balance is not part of "how we do business," it will not last.

A good place to start is with consideration of the organization's role in facilitating the deepest and most fundamental level of balance: self-realization. Self-realization refers to the individual's constructing a life and an approach to the world that reflects and honors his or her deep visions, values, and goals. At the organizational level, it has to do with how an organization can integrate individuals' self-realization with the optimization of its own effectiveness in reaching its goals.

Phase 4: Vision of the Integration between Organizational Aspirations and Human Development

Establishing a sustainable vision involves discussion throughout the organization to gain a shared sense of how fostering the self-realization of individuals fits integrally with optimal organizational functioning. Exercise 6.1 provides a list of questions around which such a dialogue can be structured.

To truly internalize such a vision requires organization members to recognize the psychological and organizational costs that ensue when managers hang their self-esteem on the precarious hook of upward ambition and promotion. A workable vision includes a recognition that diverse individual aspirations and developmental directions can be sources of tremendous energy and competitive potential. It includes an appreciation of the value of a population of leaders who are focused on the intrinsic satisfaction, involvement, and challenge of their work. It means seeing individuals' achievement of insight and development toward their deepest values as significant goals—on a par with the goal of organizational effectiveness. Furthermore, it means harnessing such development for organizational purposes, so that individuals use their talents and gifts in the service of the business while they satisfy personal growth needs. Within this vision, one function of the organization is to serve as a forum for human development.

If organizational members choose to value and support individual development toward personal goals in a way that is synergistic with organizational effectiveness, that places implied value on a wide range of intimacy- and mastery-oriented leadership and management qualities.

Phase 5: Vision of the Desired Leadership Culture

Again, as in the previous phase, we must involve many people from all over the organization in conversations about what they want

Exercise 6.1. Dialogue for Envisioning a Culture Integrating Organizational Aspirations and Human Development.

1. What does our assessment tell us about how our organization currently operates around this issue? Specifically, how do we treat people's development in the context of organizational effectiveness?

2. What are the implications, costs, and benefits of this approach to people's development—for them and for the organization?

3. How will operating in ways more supportive of balance fit with our effectiveness as an organization? For example, how does fostering self-realization enhance the following:

    - customer service
    - quality
    - productivity
    - profitability
    - human resource development
    - corporate social and environmental responsibility

4. Projecting ourselves ten years into the future, what does our self-realizing organization look like? What are people doing? What are they thinking? How do they feel? How do they treat each other? What are the sources of our effectiveness as an organization and how do they relate to our focus on the organization as a forum for people's value- and vision-based development?

from their leadership and what kinds of leaders they themselves want to be. We must also tie the desired leadership profile directly to improving the organization's ability to do its work well. Thus, we and our network of balance supporters must come to grips with the question of how a wide range of intimacy- and mastery-oriented skills and qualities, reflecting individuals' own developmental paths, serves organizational goals. For example, intimacy-oriented qualities equip managers to reflect on themselves and their needs and desires; they also equip managers to foster their direct reports' self-awareness and development. Exercise 6.2 lists questions for structuring such dialogue.

Phase 6: Vision of the Organization's Place in the Individual's Life Structure of Balanced Commitments

Let us consider what happens if a vision is established in which the organization becomes a vehicle for human development, and in fact supports the development of a wide range of leadership qualities consistent with people's rounded growth and the organization's effectiveness. It follows that new formulations are needed regarding the position of work in the executive's or manager's life and the expectations that are reasonable regarding the leaders' level of commitment to work. If the vision is durable, the workplace will be seen as just one of the interlocking parts of a manager's or an executive's life, and balanced commitments that enrich a manager's or executive's contribution to work will be seen as valuable. Exercise 6.3 suggests questions to discuss in developing this vision.

As you have reflected on the phases of organizational change, some possible strategies for implementing them probably have suggested themselves. Let's move on now to that topic.

Change Strategies

When we think about how best to initiate changes to create organizational balance, the best place to start may be our own behavior as leaders and role models. We can accomplish much toward organizational balance immediately, simply by choosing to act on our

**Exercise 6.2. Dialogue for Envisioning a Mastery- and
Intimacy-Balanced Leadership Profile.**

1. What does our assessment tell us about how our organization currently operates around this issue? Specifically, what balance of mastery- and intimacy-oriented leadership behavior do we promote?

2. What are the implications, costs, and benefits of this leadership profile for people and for the organization?

3. How will operating in ways more supportive of balance fit with our effectiveness as an organization? For example, how does a balanced leadership profile fit with the following:

    - customer service
    - quality
    - productivity
    - profitability
    - human resource development
    - corporate social and environmental responsibility

4. Projecting ourselves ten years into the future, what does our leadership-balanced organization look like? What are people doing? What are they thinking? How do they feel? How do they treat each other? What are the sources of our effectiveness as an organization and how do they relate to having an approach to leadership that balances mastery and intimacy?

Exercise 6.3. Dialogue for Building a Vision of Balanced Time, Energy, and Commitment.

1. What does our assessment tell us about how our organization currently operates around this issue? Specifically, what distribution of time, energy, and commitment do we promote?

2. What are the implications, costs, and benefits of this time/energy distribution for people and for the organization?

3. How will operating in ways more supportive of balance fit with our effectiveness as an organization? For example, how does time/energy balance fit with the following:

    *   customer service
    *   quality
    *   productivity
    *   profitability
    *   human resource development
    *   corporate social and environmental responsibility

4. Projecting ourselves ten years into the future, what does our time/ energy balanced organization look like? What are people doing? What are they thinking? How do they feel? How do they treat each other? What are the sources of our effectiveness as an organization and how do they relate to time/energy balance?

beliefs on an ongoing basis; by doing so we can also remain true to the visions and development goals we have established for ourselves as human beings.

The actions we take can create a climate where balance is possible. First, we can initiate dialogue around the issue of balance. That will help to legitimize balance as a relevant organizational concern that is linked with effectiveness. Second, we can serve as role models by visibly living balance. To the extent that we occupy influential positions (and all of us have some sphere of influence), our living consistently with balance will send messages regarding what kind of behavior is legitimate and appropriate for those who want to do well in their work and in their life. Third, we can treat our direct reports and colleagues in ways that support their pursuit of balance. And finally, to the extent that it is in our control, we can advocate and implement human resource practices that support balance—practices such as training and development programs and processes, performance standards and measures, selection and succession systems, and career planning and development systems. To a significant extent, we may not be able to design and implement such initiatives on our own, which brings us to the aspect of making change that goes beyond what we can do as individuals.

We need to continue to involve people in the organization in the growing network of balance advocates, where they can provide ideas and plans. Involving people in the development of change strategies can itself be an intervention toward balance, as well as a force to mobilize widespread commitment to change toward balance. And organizational members are likely to be valuable sources of insight regarding potential interventions and approaches. Thus, we can pull together groups of people from across the organization to identify the key balance issues they see in the organization, to create a shared vision of the balanced organization they wish to move toward, and to think of ways to address those issues and move toward the envisioned future.

Phase 7: Strategies for Encouraging Managers to Balance Work and Other Priority Commitments

The objective in this phase is to create an organizational climate that supports executives' and managers' attempts to balance their

Exercise 6.4. Sample Change Strategies for Creating a Climate for Balanced Time, Energy, and Commitment.

1. *Create dialogue.*

   Talk, and encourage others to talk, about time/energy issues you and they face.

   Talk about the importance of balanced commitments to organizational effectiveness.

2. *Be a role model.*

   Demonstrate balanced allocation of time and energy. Don't be in the office, or generating memos and E-mail from your house, on evenings and weekends.

   Say no to after-hours commitments when important personal life events conflict.

   Talk openly and candidly about your attempts at balancing commitments.

   Support your direct reports' attempts to lead balanced lives.

3. *Treat your direct reports in ways that support balance.*

   Help your direct reports set boundaries around their work, particularly when you see them becoming stressed and overloaded.

   Encourage your direct reports to discuss workload and balance issues with you.

   Encourage your direct reports to take their full vacations and otherwise take care of themselves.

   Focus on the results people produce, not the hours they put in.

   Keep an eye on your direct reports' workloads, the range and diversity of their roles and responsibilities, and their travel schedules to see that they are reasonable.

   Consider a direct report's staying at work late on a regular basis as a danger sign.

   Arrange meetings and trips so they don't involve weekend travel.

   Avoid telephoning direct reports after hours and setting up after-hours meetings.

   When direct reports come to you to discuss work–personal life conflicts, reinforce them for doing so; try to be sensitive to their issues and discuss them openly.

**Exercise 6.4. Sample Change Strategies for Creating a Climate
for Balanced Time, Energy, and Commitment, Cont'd.**

4. *Establish supportive human resource policies, systems, and structures.*

    a. *Training and development:*

    Offer workshops and seminars that help people learn strategies for
    coping with conflicting demands. For example: managing stress;
    setting boundaries; managing the transition between work and
    home; delegation, prioritization, and other work-load control
    strategies.

    Offer workshops and seminars that help people learn ways of sup-
    porting their direct reports in balancing their commitments. For
    example: dealing sensitively with the range of family care issues
    faced by people in different life situations; applying the com-
    pany's work-family policies equitably.

    Offer workshops and seminars that help employees and their fam-
    ilies manage the challenges of relocation.

    b. *Performance standards, measures, and rewards:*

    Establish performance expectations in which a balanced approach
    to work commitment is a positive standard.

    Reward supervisors for supporting balance among their direct
    reports.

    c. *Work policies:*

    Issue a formal statement from top management saying that work
    should be conducted during working hours and that employees
    should not be telephoned at home after hours, except for
    emergencies.

    Establish a policy that bars company-sponsored meetings requir-
    ing travel from being held on Mondays or Fridays.

    In travel-heavy companies, establish Fridays as "office days."

    d. *Selection and promotion:*

    Establish an interactive process for making transfer and promo-
    tion decisions so that employees can have a real say in decisions
    requiring relocation, and so that refusing a transfer or promotion
    is not penalized.

    Bring family members into discussions pertaining to potential job
    transfers and relocations.

    Provide spouses and intimate others with relocation job
    assistance.

Exercise 6.4. Sample Change Strategies for Creating a Climate for Balanced Time, Energy, and Commitment, Cont'd.

---

5. *Build an expanding network of balance supporters.*

   Look for people who express interest in family-friendly policies.

6. *Involve others in designing change.*

Source: Balancing Act, by Joan Kofodimos. Copyright © 1993 by Jossey-Bass Publishers. Permission to reproduce and distribute material, with © notice visible, is hereby granted. If material is to be used in a compilation that is for profit, please contact the publisher for permission.

time, energy, and commitment between work and personal life. As we have seen, there are many actions we can take to contribute to this climate, such as giving our own personal life high priority and helping our direct reports to set boundaries on their work.

Exercise 6.4 lists a number of actions we can take as individuals as well as some that can be initiated with broader involvement. This list can be used to spur discussion among groups of organization members, who can develop their own lists of change strategies based on the salient balance problems they have identified in their organizational assessments.

Phase 8: Strategies for Encouraging a Balance of Mastery- and Intimacy-Oriented Leadership Qualities

The objective in Phase 8 is to create a climate supportive of a leadership profile that includes both intimacy- and mastery-oriented behaviors and that takes a unique form for each individual leader according to that person's special talents and preferences. Each of us can begin to create such a climate simply by acting on our own leadership profile, derived from our values and visions for ourselves. More broadly, we can establish leadership training programs and competency models that define leadership in this new way. Exercise 6.5 suggests more sample change strategies that can be used by groups as a starting point to develop their own goals and plans.

**Exercise 6.5. Sample Change Strategies for Creating a Climate
for a Balanced Leadership Profile.**

---

1. *Create dialogue.*

    Talk about the importance of a balance between mastery- and
    intimacy-related leadership qualities.

2. *Be a role model.*

    Based on your own plans and visions for development, use your own
    unique pattern of intimacy- and mastery-oriented leadership
    behaviors.

3. *Treat your direct reports in ways that support balance.*

    Encourage direct reports to collaborate, share their doubts, support
    each other, and express other intimacy-oriented behaviors.

    Provide ongoing coaching and support in the concrete, day-to-day use
    of intimacy-oriented skills and behaviors.

4. *Establish supportive human resource policies, systems, and structures.*

    a. *Training and development:*

        Use or design management training and development programs
        that are oriented toward intimacy/mastery balance.

        Establish competency models based on a balanced leadership
        profile.

    b. *Performance standards and measures:*

        Incorporate intimacy-oriented standards and outcomes into mea-
        surement and appraisal systems. Reward and measure managers
        for demonstrating balanced leadership.

    c. *Selection and promotion systems:*

        Incorporate a balance of intimacy- and mastery-oriented qualities
        into managerial selection criteria. Think about the intimacy-
        related skills that managerial jobs require.

5. *Build an expanding network.*

    Look for others who are considered "people" managers; seek their
    support and commitment.

6. *Involve others in designing change.*

Exercise 6.6. Sample Change Strategies for Creating a Climate for Self-Realization.

1. *Create dialogue.*

   Talk about the relationship between self-realization and balance.

   Initiate discussions about new ways of thinking of success and self-worth that challenge upward-oriented models and assumptions.

2. *Be a role model.*

   Act empowered; challenge organizational actions that conflict with your beliefs and values.

   Talk about your development in terms that go beyond the career rungs you have climbed.

3. *Treat your supervisees in ways that support balance.*

   Get your direct reports involved in the design of their work.

   Let people know clearly what behaviors and outcomes will be rewarded. Try to be consistent in the various roles and expectations you place on individuals.

   Give straightforward information to people regarding their performance and potential.

   Collaborate with your direct reports to design their work so it is maximally developmental for them. Get to know them; the kinds of development they want; the new competencies and skills they want to build; the experiences, roles, and activities they want to try; the talents they want to utilize. Do development planning and goal setting within the context of their current jobs.

4. *Establish supportive human resource policies, systems, and structures.*

   a. *Training and development:*

   Involve people in identifying the performance areas in which they need development.

   Build management development experiences around self-assessment. Focus on identifying individuals' skills, interests, values, goals, competencies, and experiences. Avoid management development programs and processes that emphasize predetermined laundry lists of capabilities.

   Emphasize development of the whole person, of which development as a manager is just a part. Incorporate personal life planning into management development and career planning.

   Include in discussions of development opportunities not only management development experiences, but also on-the-job experiences and outside opportunities, such as volunteer work.

**Exercise 6.6. Sample Change Strategies for Creating
a Climate for Self-Realization, Cont'd.**

Offer workshops on asserting control over one's career.

b. *Career planning and development:*

Design systems that emphasize self-development and ongoing learning.

Offer a range of alternative paths or tracks; encourage managers and executives to design their careers so they can focus on and be rewarded for what is most satisfying to them.

Encourage the view that career paths are changeable: individuals can and should be expected to redefine their career plans and aspirations as they are affected by life experiences.

Encourage lateral movement. It provides opportunities to experience different approaches, problems, and solutions. It provides the individual with a broadened perspective and wide range of skills that are good for the company and the individual. It gives young managers a better idea of the range of potential career paths.

Provide entrepreneurial opportunities. Give people opportunities to start up new ventures in the organization or outside.

Encourage sabbaticals. These might be used for volunteer work, education, social service, travel, or long management development programs. They can be paid or unpaid, and range in length from two months to a year or more. They give managers a chance to recharge, regain perspective, expand horizons, feel rewarded. And the organization gets back a more skilled person.

Offer technical tracks that reward people with what they value (for example, increased latitude and budgets), and pay them based on the scope of their work rather than on management duties.

c. *Performance standards and measures:*

Redefine performance appraisal to better reflect the appraisee's own criteria.

d. *Reward systems:*

Compensate people for skills rather than position.

Compensate people for quality of performance rather than potential or seniority.

**Exercise 6.6. Sample Change Strategies for Creating
a Climate for Self-Realization, Cont'd.**

5. *Build an expanding network.*

6. *Involve others in designing change.*

Source: Balancing Act, by Joan Kofodimos. Copyright © 1993 by Jossey-Bass Publishers. Permission to reproduce and distribute material, with © notice visible, is hereby granted. If material is to be used in a compilation that is for profit, please contact the publisher for permission.

Phase 9: Strategies for Supporting the Pursuit of Personal Values and Missions Through Work

In Phase 9, the objective is to create an organizational climate that supports self-realization. There are a number of individual actions we can take to encourage this change; we can take charge of our own development in this manner and support our direct reports in doing so. Perhaps more important are the systemic changes we can make, in such areas as management development, participative work design, and career planning.

Exercise 6.6 provides a sample list. Here, in particular, the process of designing change must be consistent with the goal: it must be designed with the involvement of all organizational members in deciding how they want to define current performance and career success over time.

The ultimate goal is to build an organization that is strong *because* it values and supports balance. A balanced organization works better in a competitive world because it brings to the surface, develops, and takes advantage of the core values, beliefs, and capabilities of its members.

afterword

The Balance Revolution

My hope is that this book will serve as a catalyst, a launching pad, for all of us to begin living and working in ways that are consistent with balance. It is clear to me that people today want life balance, but we must free ourselves from the forces that militate against it—both our inner histories and the social structures and norms surrounding us.

It should be apparent by now that work–personal life imbalance is symptomatic of social pathology and that addressing imbalance is tantamount to addressing many of the phenomena that ail us. As with other social ills, no easy solution is to be found, but the answer most likely lies in a combination of changing the parenting practices that produce imbalanced people and changing the environment that perpetuates them. At the risk of grandiosity, we might say that what is needed for life balance is what our planet needs for survival.

Balance is in danger, however, of becoming the latest fad, a marketing slogan aligned with the collective attitudes of baby boomers. A recent advertisement from a major computer manufacturer shows a man typing at his computer in an impossibly neat house with a toddler on his shoulders, crayon drawings on the wall behind them. The text suggests that the computer was created to be a vehicle for balancing life and work.

Rather than the latest lifestyle trend, balance needs to become part of a revolution in how we live our lives. That is the same revolution that has forced us to contend with delayering, downsizing, and drastically reduced promotion opportunities as standard operating procedures and that has given us the continuous learning, high-involvement organization as the wave of the future. The kinds of changes that will support and enhance balance are consistent with the key challenges that we as individuals and organizations will face over future years.

Because we stand on this cusp between past and future, some of what has been discussed in this book has not been fully realized, particularly the comprehensive organizational changes. Some relatively small companies have been founded on balance-oriented values, such as Ben and Jerry's and The Body Shop. But what about organizations trying to move from traditional corporate values toward values that support balance? Is it possible?

This book reflects work in progress, and represents the state of my understanding at one point in a continuing evolution of insight—thus it is not intended to serve as any kind of final or complete knowledge. For this reason, I welcome your feedback and stories regarding your efforts to put balance into practice. Perhaps we can create our own community of balance advocates who can further our knowledge about the dynamics of work–personal life balance at the same time that we create constructive change in ourselves and our organizations.

If we believe in the new balanced paradigm that has been described in this book, we all must become part of the movement towards that new paradigm. At this critical juncture in our history, we have an unprecedented opportunity to reshape organizations in ways that are more humane and more effective. Whether balance is ultimately remembered as a passing fad or as the first wave in a revolution is up to each and all of us.

The Research

The insights presented in this book were initially formulated during a long-term action research study about executive character and development, which was conducted at the Center for Creative Leadership (CCL) in Greensboro, North Carolina, by Robert Kaplan, Wilfred Drath, and myself between 1982 and 1988. We wanted to know how executives' personalities and inner lives—what we called "character"—affected their leadership behavior.[1] We conducted a number of intensive clinical studies of individual executives who were either referred by their organizations or self-selected to receive feedback and coaching to boost their effectiveness. In collecting data to feed back, we interviewed the executives themselves, as well as their co-workers, families, and friends; we thus obtained a range of perspectives on each executive's managerial approach, life and career history, and personal life. We also used psychological instruments and measures to assess each subject's managerial profile and personality.[2]

In doing that work, it became apparent to me that character shaped not only leadership style but also the way individuals structured their lives and handled the relationship between their work and personal lives. I first formulated the balance framework I'll describe here in my doctoral dissertation, a biographical case study of one executive, in which I focused on the forces in his character and life history that affected his leadership strengths and weaknesses, as well as the state of his personal life.[3] As we conducted further studies to reach a total of about forty executives (including two women), I found that the patterns in his character were shared by many of the other executives with whom we worked. This additional data has allowed me to expand and refine the theory, and those findings supply the basis for many of the ideas in this book.

Meanwhile, another study was ongoing at CCL: an investigation of growth and learning in managers' lives. This study of eighty-six high-potential managers from four corporations (eighty-four men and two women), looked at the key events in managers' lives that produced lasting and significant lessons.[4] As part of this larger project, I investigated incidents of crisis in personal life and how they affected the way managers subsequently restructured their lives.[5]

After these studies were completed, I conducted organizational action research studies inquiring into the systemic forces contributing to imbalance among senior managers in two professional firms (with approximately equal numbers of men and women in each population). Furthermore, these projects involved working with the organizations to design and implement interventions in policy and practice that would lead to balanced cultures. The components of my model that describe organizational phenomena underlying imbalance emerged from these studies.

Finally, as a consultant, I have worked with a number of individuals and organizations on the question of balance. Through this work, I have sought to understand the organizational and personal forces shaping executives' and managers' life structures and levels of fulfillment. As I have talked with people about the pressures and dilemmas they face in balancing their lives, and as I have tried to find ways to help organizations diagnose and intervene in the sources of imbalance, I have gained further insight to support and explicate my arguments.

I continue to collect data from my work with organizations; this information helps in the ongoing evolution of my thinking. Readers who have experiences or anecdotes to share are encouraged to do so.

NOTES

Introduction

1. Dreyfus, L. "New Trend: Turn On to Fun, Tune In to Friends, Drop Out of the Rat Race." *Greensboro News and Record*, Feb. 24, 1991, p. G4.
2. Stanush, M. "Executive Decision: Family Life Taking Top Priority." *Austin American Statesman*, Sept. 16, 1990.
3. Saltzman, A. "Corporate Commandos Slow Down on Fast Track." *Seattle Times*, Oct. 7, 1990, p. E1.
4. Trost, K., and Hymowitz, C. "Careers Start Giving In to Family Needs." *Wall Street Journal*, June 18, 1990.
5. This survey by Yankelovich Clancy Shulman is discussed in Saltzman, "Corporate Commandos."
6. *Roper Reports 91-10.* New York: Roper Organization, 1991.
7. Levinson, D. J., and others. *The Seasons of a Man's Life.* New York: Ballantine, 1978.
8. Schor, J. B. *The Overworked American: The Unexpected Decline of Leisure.* New York: Basic Books, 1991; and Shames, L. *The Hunger for More: Searching for Values in an Age of Greed.* New York: Times Books, 1986.
9. Schlesinger, A. "The Turn of the Cycle." *New Yorker*, Nov. 16, 1992, pp. 46-54.
10. Evans, P., and Bartolome, F. *Must Success Cost So Much?* New York: Basic Books, 1981.

Chapter One

1. Bailyn, L. "The Apprenticeship Model of Organizational Careers: A Response to Changes in the Relation Between Work and Family." In P. A. Wallace (ed.), *Women in the Workplace.* Boston: Auburn House, 1982.

2. Nulty, P. "Why Do We Travel So *&!?# Much?" *Fortune,* March 28, 1988, p. 88.

3. Brett, J. M. "Job Transfer and Well-Being." *Journal of Applied Psychology,* 1982, *67* (4), 450–463.

4. Marks, S. "Multiple Roles and Role Strain: Some Notes on Human Energy, Time, and Commitment." *American Sociological Review,* 1977, *42* (Dec.), 921–936.

5. Payton-Miyazaki, M., and Brayfield, H. "The Good Job and the Good Life: The Relation of Characteristics of Employment to General Well-Being." In H. D. Biderman and T. F. Drury (eds.), *Measuring Work Quality for Social Reporting.* New York: Halstead, 1976.

6. Evans and Bartolome, *Must Success Cost So Much?,* 11.

7. Lofquist, L. H., and Dawis, R. V. *Adjustment to Work: A Psychological View of Man's Problems in a Work-Oriented Society.* New York: Appleton-Century-Crofts, 1969.

8. Lasch, C. *The Culture of Narcissism.* New York: Norton, 1978.

9. Edwards, J. *The Works of President Edwards.* Vol. IV. New York: Robert Carter and Brothers, 1879.

10. Peters, T., and Austin, N. *A Passion for Excellence.* New York: Warner Books, 1985, 495–496.

11. Schaef, A. W., and Fassel, D. *The Addictive Organization.* New York: Harper & Row, 1988.

12. Kanter, R. *Men and Women of the Corporation.* New York: Basic Books, 1977, 105. See also R. Seidenberg, *Corporate Wives—Corporate Casualties?* New York: AMACOM, 1973.

13. Papenek, H. "Men, Women, and Work: Reflections on the Two-Person Single Career." *American Journal of Sociology,* 1973, *78,* 852–872.

14. Bailyn, L. "Career and Family Orientations of Husbands and

Wives in Relation to Marital Happiness." *Human Relations,*
1970, *23,* 97–113.

15. Morrison, A. M., White, R. P., and Van Velsor, E. *Breaking
the Glass Ceiling: Can Women Make It to the Top in America's Top Corporations?* Reading, Mass.: Addison-Wesley,
1987, 114.

16. Morrison, White, and Van Velsor, *Breaking the Glass Ceiling.*

17. A number of sources have contributed to the conclusions in
this paragraph: Burke, R., and Weir, T. "Impact of Occupational Demands on Nonwork Experiences. *Group and Organization Studies,* 1981, *6* (4), 472–485; Bray, D., Campbell, R.,
and Grant, D. *Formative Years in Business: A Long-Term
AT&T Study of Managerial Lives.* New York: Wiley-
Interscience, 1974; Grieff, B., and Munter, P. *Tradeoffs: Executive, Family, and Organizational Life.* New York: New
American Library, 1980; and Schaef and Fassel, *The Addictive
Organization.*

18. Schaef and Fassel, *The Addictive Organization;* Faunce, W.,
and Dubin, R. "Individual Investment in Working and Living." In L. Davis and A. Cherns (eds.), *The Quality of Working Life.* Vol. 1. New York: Free Press, 1975; Bartolome, F.
"The Work Alibi: When It's Harder to Go Home." *Harvard
Business Review,* March-April, 1983.

19. Rohrlich, J. *Work and Love: The Crucial Balance.* New York:
Harmony Books, 1980.

20. Nulty, P. "Why Do We Travel So *&!?# Much?" p. 88.

21. Korman, A., and Korman, R. *Career Success/Personal Failure.*
Englewood Cliffs, N.J.: Prentice-Hall, 1980.

22. Allen, F. "Executives' Wives Describe Sources of Their Contentment, Frustration." *Wall Street Journal,* Dec. 15, 1981,
p. 29.

23. Adams, J. "Conversation with a Successful Man." *Across the
Board,* April 1982, pp. 49–50.

24. Cleveland, H. *The Future Executive: A Guide for Tomorrow's
Managers.* Harper & Row, 1972.

25. Marks, "Multiple Roles and Role Strain"; Lobel, S. A. "Allocation of Investment in Work and Family Roles: Alternative

Theories and Implications for Research." *Academy of Management Review*, 1991, *16* (3), 507–521.

Chapter Two

1. Kegan, R. *The Evolving Self: Problem and Process in Human Development.* Cambridge, Mass.: Harvard University Press, 1982, 107.

2. Baruch, G., Barnett, R., and Rivers, C. *Life Prints: New Patterns of Love and Work for Today's Women.* New York: New American Library, 1983; Bakan, D. *The Duality of Human Existence.* Boston: Beacon Press, 1966; Lyons, N. P., Saltonstall, J. F., and Hanmer, T. J. "Competencies and Visions." In C. Gilligan, N. P. Lyons, and T. J. Hanmer (eds.), *Making Connections: The Relational Worlds of Adolescent Girls at Emma Willard School.* Cambridge, Mass.: Harvard University Press, 1990. Smelser, N. J. "Vicissitudes of Work and Love in Anglo-American Society. In N. J. Smelser and E. H. Erikson (eds.), *Themes of Work and Love in Adulthood.* Cambridge, Mass.: Harvard University Press, 1980, 105–119.

3. Mullahy, P. "The Theories of H. S. Sullivan." In H. Sullivan (ed.), *The Contributions of Harry Stack Sullivan.* New York: Hermitage House, 1952, 13–59; Hendrick, I. "Work and the Pleasure Principle." *Psychoanalytic Quarterly*, 1943, *12*, 311–329; Becker, E. *Angel in Armor.* New York: George Braziller, 1969.

4. Rohrlich, *Work and Love;* and Stern, K. *The Flight from Woman.* New York: Noonday Press, 1965.

5. Gallos, J. V. "Exploring Women's Development: Implications for Career Theory, Practice, and Research." In M. B. Arthur, D. T. Hall, and B. S. Lawrence (eds.), *Handbook of Career Theory.* Cambridge: Cambridge University Press, 1989, 110–132.

6. Morrison, White, and Van Velsor, *Breaking the Glass Ceiling,* p. 50.

7. Maccoby, M. "The Corporate Climber Has to Find His Heart." In M.F.R. Kets de Vries (ed.), *The Irrational Execu-*

tive: Psychoanalytic Explorations in Management. Madison, Conn.: International Universities Press, 1984, 96–111.

8. See, for example, Bennis, W., and Nanus, B. *Leaders: The Strategies for Taking Charge.* New York: Harper & Row, 1985.
9. May, R. *Love and Will.* New York: Norton, 1969, 277.
10. Levinson, H. *Executive Stress.* New York: New American Library, 1975.
11. May, R. *Man's Search for Himself.* New York: Dell, 1969, 117.
12. Becker, *Angel in Armor*, 83–85.
13. Robinson, B. E. *Work Addiction: Hidden Legacies of Adult Children.* Deerfield Beach, Fla.: Health Communications, Inc., 1989.

Chapter Three

1. Horney, K. *Neurosis and Human Growth.* New York: Norton, 1950.
2. Miller, A. *The Drama of the Gifted Child.* New York: Basic Books, 1981.
3. Rogers, C. R. *Client-Centered Therapy.* Boston: Houghton Mifflin, 1951.
4. Horney, *Neurosis and Human Growth*, 9.
5. Jung, C. G. "Excerpt from the Relations Between the Ego and the Unconscious." In J. Campbell (ed.), *The Portable Jung.* New York: Penguin Books, 1959, 70–138. (Originally published 1928.)
6. Kohut, H. *The Analysis of Self: A Systemic Approach to the Psychoanalytic Treatment of Narcissistic Personality Disorders.* Madison, Conn.: International Universities Press, 1971.
7. Horney, *Neurosis and Human Growth*, 202–203.
8. Jourard, S. M. *The Transparent Self.* New York: Van Nostrand Reinhold, 1964; Miller, *The Drama of the Gifted Child.*
9. Horney, *Neurosis and Human Growth.*
10. Henry, W. E. "The Business Executive: The Psychodynamics of a Social Role." *American Journal of Sociology*, 1949, *54*, 286–291.
11. Henry, "The Business Executive," p. 289.

12. Schwartz, H. S. "Organizational Motivation and the Dark Side of Organizational Life." Paper presented at American Academy of Management, Miami Beach, August 1991.

13. Jackall, R. *Moral Mazes: The World of Corporate Managers.* New York: Oxford University Press, 1988.

14. Kaplan, R. E., Drath, W. H., and Kofodimos, J. R. "High Hurdles: The Challenge of Executive Self-Development." Technical Report. Greensboro, N.C.: Center for Creative Leadership, 1985.

15. LaBier, D. *Modern Madness: The Emotional Fallout of Success.* Reading, Mass.: Addison-Wesley, 1986.

16. Gruen, A. *The Betrayal of the Self: The Fear of Autonomy in Men and Women.* New York: Grove Press, 1988.

17. Hall, D. T., and Richter, J. "Career Gridlock: Baby Boomers Hit the Wall." *Academy of Management Executive,* 1990, *4* (3), pp. 7–22; Weick, K. E., and Berlinger, L. R. "Career Improvisation in Self-Designing Organizations." In M. B. Arthur, D. T. Hall, and B. S. Lawrence (eds.), *Handbook of Career Theory.* Cambridge: Cambridge University Press, 1989, 313–328.

Chapter Four

1. Garfield, C. *Second to None: Business in the Ecological Age.* Keynote address at the First International Conference of the Institute of Noetic Sciences, Santa Clara, California, June 1992.

2. Vaill, P. B. *Managing as a Performing Art: New Ideas for a World of Chaotic Change.* San Francisco: Jossey-Bass, 1989, 2.

3. Katz, S. J., and Liu, A. E. *Success Trap.* New York: Dell, 1990.

4. Kaplan, R. E. "Character Shifts: The Challenge of Improving Executive Performance Through Personal Growth." Technical Report. Greensboro, N.C.: Center for Creative Leadership, 1990.

Chapter Five

1. Kaplan, R. E., Drath, W. H., and Kofodimos, J. R. *Beyond Ambition: How Driven Managers Can Lead Better and Live Better.* San Francisco: Jossey-Bass, 1991.

2. Streufert, S. "The Stress of Excellence: Why Our Best Decision Makers May Face the Greatest Risk of Heart Attacks." *Across the Board,* Oct. 1983, pp. 8-16.

3. Kiechel, W., III. "When Executives Crack." *Fortune,* July 23, 1984, pp. 133-134.

4. Rohrlich, *Work and Love.*

5. *Penetration,* a term that refers to the ways in which executives stay informed about the activities in their organization, was first used by Wilfred Drath at the Center for Creative Leadership.

6. McClelland, D. C. "The Two Faces of Power." In D. A. Kolb, I. M. Rubin, and J. M. McIntyre (eds.), *Organizational Psychology.* Englewood Cliffs, N.J.: Prentice-Hall, 1984, 141-154.

7. Slater, P. *A Dream Deferred: America's Discontent and the Search for a New Democratic Ideal.* Boston: Beacon Press, 1991.

8. Jackall, *Moral Mazes.*

9. Gordon, S. "A National Care Agenda." *Atlantic Monthly,* Jan. 1991, pp. 64-68.

10. Lobel, S. A., Dutton, J. E., and O'Neill, R. "Nurturing: Elaborating Our Understanding of Important Roles, Skills, and Contexts in Organizations." Paper presented at the Eighth Annual Conference of Women and Work, May 7-8, 1992, Arlington, Texas.

11. Bragar, J. L. "Effective Leadership Practices for Managers: Balancing Interdependence and Autonomy. Doctoral dissertation, Harvard University Graduate School of Education, 1990.

12. Bragar, "Effective Leadership Practices," 85.

Chapter Six

1. Hall, D. T., and Richter, J. "Balancing Work Life and Home Life: What Can Organizations Do to Help?" *Academy of Management Executive,* 1988, 2 (3), 213-223.

Appendix

1. The findings of the broader study are reported in the following works: Kaplan, Drath, and Kofodimos, "High Hurdles";

Kofodimos, J. R., Kaplan, R. E., and Drath, W. H. "Anatomy of an Executive: A Close Look at One Executive's Managerial Character and Development." Technical Report. Greensboro, N.C.: Center for Creative Leadership, 1986; Kaplan, Drath, and Kofodimos, *Beyond Ambition.*

2. For a description of our intensive methodology, biographical action research, see Kofodimos, J. R., "Using Biographical Methods to Understand Managerial Style and Character." *Journal of Applied Behavioral Science,* 1990, *26* (4), 433–459.

3. Kofodimos, J. R. "Paul Simmons, Executive: A Psychological Biography." Doctoral dissertation, Yale University, 1986.

4. McCall, M. W., Lombardo, M. M., and Morrison, A. M. *The Lessons of Experience: How Successful Executives Develop on the Job.* Lexington, Mass.: Lexington Books, 1988.

5. Kofodimos, J. R. *A Question of Balance.* Issues and Observations, vol. 4, no. 1. Greensboro, NC: Center for Creative Leadership, 1984.

INDEX